What I Am Living For

"A kind of everysoul, Merton possessed an extraordinary ability to connect with deep, universal places inside of people."

Sue Monk Kidd
Author of *The Secret Life of Bees*

"Merton calls us to acknowledge what is deepest and most mysterious in all of us, even as he reminds us that we can't disappear into a cloud of piety, above it all."

Pico Iyer
Author of *The Art of Stillness*

"An extraordinary gathering of diverse voices vividly articulates Merton's deep impact on a generation of honorable readers. Gleaning profound spiritual life lessons from the monk's art of confession and witness, these reflections by contemplative educators—writing beautifully here out of the roots of their own lives—perfectly commemorate the fiftieth anniversary of the death of a master teacher."

Jonathan Montaldo
Editor of *The Intimate Merton*

"Thomas Merton lovers, rejoice: this collection is a welcome addition to your library, with essays on Merton that are by turns inspiring, enlightening, challenging, eloquent, and bracing. I hope and pray this will introduce a new generation of readers to a man who has influenced countless believers (including this one!). *What I Am Living For* reminds us why Thomas Merton remains one of the most influential and compelling spiritual writers of the twentieth century—and why he has much to say to readers in the twenty-first."

Deacon Greg Kandra
Blogger and journalist at *Aleteia*

"Classics are works that endure over time. These essays by contemporary spiritual teachers from Buddhist, Jewish, and Christian traditions reflect on the continuing influence of Merton's life and writing. New and experienced readers of Merton will find the reflections moving and Merton's views classically pertinent."

Bonnie Thurston
Founding member and past president of the
International Thomas Merton Society

What I Am Living For

lessons from the life and writings of
Thomas Merton

CONTRIBUTORS INCLUDE:
Robert Barron
Sylvia Boorstein
Robert Ellsberg
Gregory K. Hillis
Daniel P. Horan, O.F.M.
Pico Iyer
Sue Monk Kidd
James Martin, S.J.
Kaya Oakes

Edited by Jon M. Sweeney

AVE MARIA PRESS AVE Notre Dame, Indiana

James Martin's essay "Becoming Who We Are" is excerpted from *Becoming Who You Are* by James Martin, S.J., copyright © 2006, HiddenSpring, an imprint of Paulist Press, Inc., New York/Mahwah, NJ, and is reprinted by permission of Paulist Press, Inc. www.paulistpress.com.

Sue Monk Kidd's essay "False Self, True Self" appeared previously as the introduction to *New Seeds of Contemplation*, copyright © 2007 New Directions, and is used by permission of the author.

Judith Simmer-Brown's essay "Merton on the Spiritual Promise of Interreligous Dialogue" was adapted by her from "Wide Open to Life: Thomas Merton's Dialogue of Contemplative Practice," *Buddhist-Christian Studies* 35 (2015): 193–203, Honolulu: University of Hawaii Press.

Founded in 1865, Ave Maria Press is a ministry of the United States Province of Holy Cross.

www.avemariapress.com

Paperback: ISBN-13 978-1-59471-741-3

E-book: ISBN-13 978-1-59471-742-0

Cover image of Thomas Merton by Sibyelle Akers. Used with permission of the Merton Legacy Trust and the Thomas Merton Center at Bellarmine University. Landscape image © Getty Images/breckeni.

Cover and text design by Samantha Watson.

Printed and bound in the United States of America

Library of Congress Cataloging-in-Publication Data is available.

If you want to identify me, ask me not where I live, or what I like to eat, or how I comb my hair, but ask me what I am living for, in detail, and ask me what I think is keeping me from living fully for the thing I want to live for.

—Thomas Merton

Contents

Chronology of Merton's Life and World Events (1915–1968)

THOMAS MERTON

1915   Born January 31 in Prades, France, son of artist parents traveling abroad. Father Owen was from New Zealand, and mother Ruth was from the United States.

1921   Ruth dies from cancer Thomas travels—in the United States, Bermuda, and France—with Owen.

1926   Enrolls in school in Montauban, France.

1928   Moves with father to England and enrolls at Ripley Court School, a year later at Oakham School in the East Midlands.

1931   Owen dies of a brain tumor. Thomas is an orphan
                at sixteen.

1932   Earns a scholarship to Clare College, Cambridge.

1934   Leaves Cambridge University, and moves to the
                United States.

1935   Enrolls at Columbia University in New York where
                he is mentored by professor Mark Van Doren.

1937   Encounters a God he can believe in after reading *The
                Spirit of Mediaeval Philosophy*, by Étienne Gilson.

1938   Graduates from Columbia and begins work on an
                master's degree, also at Columbia.

1938   In September is moved by an account of the conver-
                sion of poet Gerard Manley Hopkins to Catholicism.
                Goes to see the priest at Corpus Christi Church,
                near Columbia. Received into the Catholic Church
                there on November 16.

1940–1941   Teaches English literature at St. Bonaventure College,
                upstate New York. Explores a Franciscan vocation.

1941   Enters the Abbey of Our Lady of Gethsemani in
                Kentucky, December 10, seeking to become a Trap-
                pist monk.

1944   Makes his simple vows.

1946   Publishes second volume of poems.

1947   Makes his solemn vows on March 19 with several friends, Catholic and literary, in attendance.

1948   His autobiography, *The Seven Storey Mountain*, is published in October and becomes one of the best-selling books in the United States the following year.

1951–1955 Serves as master of scholastics at the monastery.

1955–1965 Serves as master of novices.

1958   A turning point in his spiritual life when he "turns toward the world" at the corner of Fourth and Walnut Streets in downtown Louisville. By this time, he is corresponding with a range of literary, religious, scholarly, and activist friends, including Boris Pasternak, Erich Fromm, Aldous Huxley, D. T. Suzuki, Rosemary Radford Ruether, Fr. Daniel Berrigan, and Rabbi Abraham Joshua Heschel.

1960   Begins to publish on issues of social justice, political controversy, and peace, including the civil rights movement and opposition to war in southeast Asia.

1965   Begins to live as a semi-hermit, still a member of the monastic community, but living apart on monastery grounds. Also publishes on Eastern religions and philosophy: *Gandhi on Non-Violence* and *The Way of Chuang Tzu* appear.

1966   Vietnamese monk Thich Nhat Hanh, exiled from his homeland, visits Thomas at Gethsemani in May.

1968   On September 10, leaves for a journey to New Mexico, Alaska, and California to visit old friends, then to the Far East in pilgrimage to Buddhist religious sites and communities, never to return home. On October 15, leaves the United States. Dies in Bangkok on December 10, alone in his room after speaking at a meeting of Benedictines and Cistercians from throughout Asia.

1973   *The Asian Journal of Thomas Merton*, including Thomas's journal entries throughout his travels to the Far East, as well as the text of his final lecture, is published.

WORLD EVENTS THAT IMPACT MERTON

1914   World War I begins.

1918   Gerard Manley Hopkins's *Poems* first published.

1927   First volume of D. T. Suzuki's *Essays in Zen Buddhism* translated into English and published in America.

1930   Novelist Evelyn Waugh (*Brideshead Revisited*, etc.) received into the Roman Catholic Church.

1933   Hitler becomes chancellor of Germany. Dorothy Day and Peter Maurin begin the Catholic Worker Movement in the United States.

1936   French Thomist Étienne Gilson's *The Spirit of Mediaeval Philosophy* is translated into English and published in America.

1941   The United States enters World War II, joining the fight against the Axis powers of Germany, Japan, and Italy.

1945   The United States drops two atomic bombs on the people of Japan, killing hundreds of thousands.

1955–1975 The United States participates in a sometimes covert, sometimes overt, war in Vietnam, Laos, and Cambodia.

1961   "Freedom Rides" of young civil rights activists begin in the American South. Many are violently attacked by people claiming Christian belief and values.

1965   Two documents, including *Declaration on the Relation of the Church to Non-Christian Religions* (*Nostra Aetate*), emerge from the Second Vatican Council on the importance of Catholics engaging in fruitful and pastoral dialogue with people of other faiths.

1968   Dr. Martin Luther King Jr. is shot and killed in Memphis. Jesuit priest Daniel Berrigan and his brother Philip burn draft notices in Catonsville, Maryland. Their statement boldly proclaims, "We confront the Roman Catholic Church, other Christian bodies, and the synagogues of America with their silence and cowardice in the face of our country's crimes."

Abbreviations

AJ   *The Asian Journal of Thomas Merton*, by Thomas Merton, edited by Patrick Hart, O.C.S.O., et al. New York: New Directions, 1975.

CGB   *Conjectures of a Guilty Bystander*, by Thomas Merton. New York: Image, 1968.

CWA   *Contemplation in a World of Action*, by Thomas Merton. Notre Dame, IN: University of Notre Dame Press, 1998.

ES   *Entering the Silence: Becoming a Monk and Writer* (*The Journals of Thomas Merton, Volume 2: 1941– 1952*), edited by Jonathan Montaldo. New York: HarperOne, 1997.

FV   *Faith and Violence*, by Thomas Merton. Notre Dame, IN: University of Notre Dame Press, 1968.

HGL   *The Hidden Ground of Love: The Letters of Thomas Merton on Religious Experience and Social Concerns*, edited by William H. Shannon. New York: Farrar, Straus & Giroux, 1986.

LIL   *Thomas Merton: A Life in Letters*, edited by William H. Shannon and Christine M. Bochen. Notre Dame, IN: Ave Maria Press, 2010.

LL   *Learning to Love: Exploring Solitude and Freedom*
        (*The Journals of Thomas Merton, Volume 6: 1966–
        1967*), edited by Christine M. Bochen. New York:
        HarperOne, 1998.

MZM   *Mystics and Zen Masters*, by Thomas Merton. New York:
        Farrar, Straus & Giroux, 1999.

NMI   *No Man Is an Island*, by Thomas Merton. New York:
        Mariner Books, 2002.

NSC   *New Seeds of Contemplation*, by Thomas Merton.
        New York: New Directions, 2007.

OSM   *The Other Side of the Mountain: The End of the Journey*
        (*The Journals of Thomas Merton, Volume 7: 1967–
        1968*), edited by Patrick Hart, O.C.S.O. New York:
        HarperOne, 1999.

RJ   *The Road to Joy: The Letters of Thomas Merton to New and
        Old Friends*, edited by Robert E. Daggy. New York:
        Mariner Books, 1993.

SFS   *Search for Solitude: Pursuing the Monk's True Life*
        (*The Journals of Thomas Merton, Volume 3: 1952–
        1960*), edited by Lawrence S. Cunningham. New
        York: HarperOne, 1997.

SJ   *The Secular Journal*, by Thomas Merton. New York:
        Noonday Press, 1977.

SOC   *The School of Charity: The Letters of Thomas Merton on
        Religious Renewal and Spiritual Direction*, edited by
        Patrick Hart, O.C.S.O. New York: Mariner Books,
        1993.

SOJ   *The Sign of Jonas*, by Thomas Merton. New York: Harvest
        Books, 2002.

SSM   *The Seven Storey Mountain*, by Thomas Merton. New York:
        Mariner Books, 1999.

TTW   *Turning toward the World: The Pivotal Years* (*The Journals of Thomas Merton, Volume 4: 1960–1963*), edited by Victor A. Kramer. New York: HarperOne, 1997.

WD   *The Wisdom of the Desert*, by Thomas Merton. New York: New Directions, 1970.

PART I

Lessons from the Life and Teachings of Thomas Merton

1.

Becoming Who We Are

JAMES MARTIN, S.J.

Thomas Merton's writings were one of the main reasons I left a job at General Electric and entered the Jesuit order in the late 1980s. A chance encounter with a television documentary on his life led me to track down and read *The Seven Storey Mountain*. But it was this quote, from *No Man Is an Island*, that stopped me dead in my tracks as an aspiring corporate executive: "Why do we have to spend our lives striving to be something that we would never want to be, if we only knew what we wanted? Why do we waste our time doing things which, if we only stopped to think about them, are just the opposite of what we were made for?" (*NMI*, 125–26).

Even after I entered the novitiate, Merton's writings continued to be a big help. His simple concept of the true self, the person we are before God and the person we are meant to be, was a critical insight in my spiritual life. His lines about "striving to be

3

something that we would never want to be" continued to be part of my daily meditation.

Overall, the quest both to understand oneself and to finally accept oneself was a key journey for me as Jesuit novice. Interestingly, the very next line after that passage I mentioned from *No Man Is an Island* is this: "We cannot become ourselves unless we know ourselves." So I set out on the quest to know myself. In fact, I had begun that journey in earnest on the day that I first started reading *The Seven Storey Mountain*. But back then, I didn't see it that way. If you had asked me, I would have probably said that I was simply trying to "escape" from my old life.

It is probably more accurate to describe what was going on as a gradual movement toward becoming the true self and away from the false self. Before coming to know the true self, one must confront the false self that one has usually spent a lifetime constructing and nourishing.

In his book *New Seeds of Contemplation*, Merton wrote, "Every one of us is shadowed by an illusory person: the false self" (*NSC*, xi). With his typical insight, Merton identifies the false self as the person that we wish to present to the world, and the person we want the whole world to revolve around:

> Thus I use up my life in the desire for pleasures and the thirst for experiences, for power, honor, knowledge and love, to clothe this false self and construct its nothingness into something objectively real. And I wind experiences around myself and cover myself with pleasures and glory like bandages in order to make myself perceptible to myself and to the world, as if I were an invisible body that could only become visible when something visible covered its surface. (*NSC*, 35)

The notion of being "clothed" with the bandages of the false self, like the Invisible Man being wrapped, mummy-like, in long, winding strips of cloth, struck a deep chord within me. The self that I had for many years presented to others—the person interested in climbing the corporate ladder, in always being clever and hip, in knowing how to order the best wines, in attending the hottest parties, and in getting into the hippest clubs, in never doubting my place in the world, in always being, in a word, *cool*—that person was unreal. That person was nothing more than a mask I wore. And I knew it.

I had known it for some time, too.

One warm day in spring, during senior year at the University of Pennsylvania's Wharton School of Business, I was walking jauntily across campus to a job interview dressed in a new suit and tie. On one level, I felt confident. Assured. Certain. Just about to finish up my degree at Wharton, I had a full slate of job interviews lined up with some of the world's biggest companies. In a few months I would be making lots of money, possibly have my own office, and be set for life. Over my arm, I was carrying an expensive new khaki raincoat that I had just bought for interviewing season.

On my way, I passed a good friend. She took one look at me and said, "Wow, you look like you're carrying a prop." I felt unmasked.

Of course, almost any college student would probably feel strange in that situation; everyone I knew felt as if they were doing a bit of playacting when it came to interviews. But my friend's words struck at a deeper level: I felt as if those bandages that I had wrapped around me had suddenly been stripped away. My heart knew that as much as I *wanted* to want this, I wasn't made for the life that I was supposed to want.

Now, I should note that business is a fine vocation for a great many people—many of my friends, in fact. The point is not that business is somehow bad, but rather that this life was pretty much the opposite of what I wanted to be doing. Yet I had created, over many years, this persona, this other self, which I thought would be pleasing to everyone: to my family, my friends, my professors.

And this "false self," separated from my true desires, was sure that a life in corporate America was the right path. This false self was sure about everything.

I love what Richard Rohr, the Franciscan priest, says about this in his book *Adam's Return*: "Our false self is who we *think* we are. It is our mental self-image and social agreement, which most people spend their whole lives living up to—or down to."

Keeping this false self alive requires a good deal of work. And for me, it was an almost all-consuming effort. It took work to convince people that I was all the things I wanted them to think I was: "Of course I can't wait to start my job!" It took work to make sure that no one saw me as uncertain about anything in life, especially in my professional life. "Of course I love reading the *Wall Street Journal*!" It took work to run away from my true desires, my true feelings, and my true vocation in life: "Of course I love my job!"

The "clothing" of yourself with these bandages, in Merton's phrase, also means that if you are not ever-vigilant, those bandages may occasionally slip and reveal your underlying true self to others. A few years after beginning my work at General Electric, I used to doodle on my desk this note, over and over, in small letters: "I hate my life." How sad it is to remember that. But it felt that this was the only way I could express myself.

A friend, sitting at my desk one evening, noticed these scribblings. It was around ten at night, and we were horsing around, laughing and throwing wadded-up pieces of paper at each other. Letting off steam after a tiring day. He glanced down at my desk. In an instant, his face dropped and a wave of pity crossed his features.

"Do you really hate your life?" he said quietly.

How strange it felt to sit across from my friend. How strange it felt for my false self to be revealed, to have the bandages slip and show my real feelings. I longed to be honest with him. There were two choices: to be honest and share myself with another person, or to lie and conceal myself from my friend. I chose the second option. "What?" I said.

He pointed to the words I had written. Looking over his shoulder, I pretended to read them for the first time. "Oh," I said, carefully rearranging the bandages of my false self, "I was just having a bad day, you know?" The false self had reasserted itself. Those bandages would not fall away for many years.

━ ━ ━ ━ ━ ━ ━ ━ ━ ━ ━

The trajectory of Merton's own life clearly shows his own steady movement away from the false self. This is perhaps most evident in his gradual acceptance and understanding of his vocation as a Trappist monk.

Merton's early journals and letters are filled with a confidence that unsuccessfully masks a deep longing for a place to belong. These feelings continue unabated until the day he enters the monastery, when he finally finds the home he has long been searching for. But even then, during his years at the abbey, even after he has become a monk, Merton continues to meditate on what *kind* of monk he is intended to be, as he moves closer toward being the person God intended him to be. His spiritual journey was far from complete when he entered the doors of the abbey. In many ways, it had just begun.

But it was not a solitary journey. Indeed, Merton speaks of this journey as "discovering myself in discovering God." Ultimately, he says, "If I find Him I will find myself, and if I find my true self I will find Him." In other words, God desires for us to be the persons we were created to be: to be simply and purely ourselves, and in this state to love God and to let ourselves be loved by God. It is a double journey, really: finding God means allowing ourselves to be found by God. And finding our true selves means allowing God to find and reveal our true selves to us.

Those spiritual phrases may sound overly abstract and overly pious, and maybe even a little hollow and hokey. What does this mean on a practical level? And how does one put that insight into action?

Simply put, we attempt to move *away* from those parts of ourselves that prevent us from being closer to God: selfishness, pride, fear, and so on. And we also try, as far as possible, to move *toward* those parts of ourselves that draw us nearer to God. In the process, we gradually find ourselves growing more loving and more generous. We also trust that the very *desire* to do this comes from God. That is, the desire for our true selves to be revealed, and for us to move nearer to God, is a desire planted within us by God.

At the same time, our own individuality, our own brand of holiness, is gradually revealed. Our personalities are not eradicated but paradoxically are made fuller, more real, and finally more holy. In his collection of essays entitled *Karl Rahner: Spiritual Writings*, the esteemed Catholic theologian wrote, "Christianity's sense of the human relationship to God is not one that says that the more a person grows closer to God, the more that person's existence vanishes into a puff of smoke."[1]

In the quest for the true self, one therefore begins to appreciate and accept one's personality and one's life as an essential way that God calls us to be ourselves. Everyone is called to sanctity in different ways—in often *very* different ways. The path to sanctity for a young mother is different from that of an elderly priest. Moreover, the path to sanctity for an extroverted young man who loves nothing more than spending time with his friends cheering on their favorite baseball team over a few beers is probably very different from that of the introspective middle-aged woman who likes nothing better than to sit at home in her favorite chair with a good book and a pot of chamomile tea. One's personal brand of holiness becomes clearer the more the true self is revealed.

And as we move closer to becoming our true selves, the selves we are meant to be, the selves that God created, the more loving parts of us are naturally magnified and the more sinful parts are naturally diminished—as are so many other blocks to true freedom. As Rohr writes, "Once you learn to live as your true self, you can never be satisfied with this charade again: it then feels so silly and superficial."

By the way, this may anticipate an important critique of the notion of the true self. Just recently, when I was discussing these notions of the true self with a fellow Jesuit, he asked, "Well, that's fine, but what happens if your true self is a horrible, lying, mean-spirited person?"

My answer was that this would not be the person God created. In other words, to find his true self, the horrible, lying, mean-spirited person would have to uncover his true self—the good self that God created—from underneath all those layers of sinfulness. And I would suspect that the longer he had been living as a selfish person, the longer it would take for him to uncover his true self.

Over the course of his life, Merton, for example, became a more expansive and generous person, and, likewise, his intolerance of others diminished over time. This was an outgrowth of his quest to be himself and to move closer to God. And it is evident in his writings.

In *The Secular Journal*, for example, the collection of journals from the late 1930s and early 1940s that immediately preceded Merton's entrance into the Trappists, the reader meets a clever young man full of enthusiasm and strongly held beliefs on literature, art, politics, people, and, in time, religion. The reader also meets a young man who is sometimes insufferably smug. (It is a testimony to Merton's humility that he allowed some of the smuggest passages to remain in his manuscript.)

There is, for example, a cringe-inducing entry detailing his visit to the New York World's Fair in 1939. In his journal, he recounts

his reactions as he observes the crowds responding to some notable paintings that have been sent over for exhibition at the fair. It
is a merciless portrait of Merton's fellow human beings, who are
depicted as far less sophisticated than the writer. He even mocks
some of them for not being able to correctly pronounce the name
of the sixteenth-century Flemish artist Peter Bruegel: "There were
a lot of people who just read the name: 'Broo-gul,' and walked on
unabashed. . . . They came across with the usual reaction of people
who don't know pictures are there to be enjoyed, but think they are
things that have to be learned by heart to impress the bourgeoisie:
so they tried to remember the name" (*SJ*, 19–20). The possibility
that among those crowds were people who appreciated what they
were seeing is entirely lost on the young Merton. The idea that he
might give them the benefit of the doubt is likewise absent.

A few years later, in *The Seven Storey Mountain*, Merton reveals
more of his youthful and occasionally patronizing attitudes, particularly when it comes to other religions. Though one could find
some "sincere charity" among Quakers, the Society of Friends is
summed up in a few dismissive lines: "But when I read the works
of William Penn and found them to be as supernatural as the
Montgomery Ward catalog, I lost interest in the Quakers" (*SSM*,
128). Ironically, Eastern spirituality, which would play a great role
in Merton's later life, is similarly dismissed. After a discussion about
his attempts at self-hypnosis, he writes, "Ultimately, I suppose all
Oriental mysticism can be reduced to techniques that do the same
thing, but in a far more subtle and advanced fashion: and if that
is true it is not mysticism at all" (*SSM*, 205). So much for *that*
spiritual tradition!

Ultimately, though, in his later years Merton recognized the
inherent beauty of all religious traditions. (And ruefully looked
back on the judgmental attitudes of his youth.) His discovery of
the true self led him to embrace not only the self that God had
created in him but also the self that God had created in others.

That gradual recognition would lead, ineluctably, to his beautiful assimilation of himself into the whole of humanity, during his famous epiphany at Fourth and Walnut in Louisville, when he perceived everyone walking around "shining like the sun" (*CGB*, 155).

2.

Meeting Thomas Merton for the First Time

Mary Neill, O.P.

It is perhaps presumptuous to include Thomas Merton in any roster of saints since he is not canonized, nor likely to be, since he was careful to write in his voluminous journals sufficient material regarding his failings, doubts, and misgivings to cheer the heart of any devil's advocate. But if a saint is someone who relentlessly searches for God and inspires others to do likewise, then Merton deserves to be included. Monica Furlong writes of him: "Yet for to those who look on, Merton seems one of the very few in the twentieth century who dared to follow in the footsteps of the saints, who revealed some of their love and self-forgetfulness (as if they had found a center outside the ego and were focused on that). He refused to be a 'dummy' for our illusions of holiness."[1]

His influence, fifty years after his death, continues to be extraordinary. Numerous biographies, doctoral dissertations, television specials, and even plays continue to pour out around this man who was and is a dividing spirit. When, at fifty-three years of age, he was electrocuted in Bangkok in 1968, on the twenty-seventh anniversary of his entrance into monastic life, there were those who saw his death as that of a saint, emblematic of his desire to serve the "burnt men" of Christ, and those who saw this bizarre death as God's punishment for dabbling in Zen and yoga—obvious works of the devil. He was and is a sign of contradiction because he attempted in his life to be a marriage broker of many opposites: European and American cultures; art and religion; medieval (monasticism) and modern consciousness; the priestly and the prophetic; the romantic and the everyday; the contemplative and the political activist; the obedient and the rebellious; passionate faith and passionate doubt; sensitivity to personal sin and occupation with social sin; strong personal independence and deep friendships; stability and restlessness. And though he had, as one person remarked, four times the psychic energy of the ordinary person, these "marriages" were often wobbly and broken, as he was the first to admit. He wore no masks of wholeness; his face—and his writings—concealed nothing. He was content to live the truth of the contraries in himself, leaving the perception of wholeness to be a hidden one, hidden in Christ with the identity, the singleness of being, that would be manifested on the last day. He wrote: "Our supernatural identity is hidden in . . . the hand of God. If we do not accept it, we shall never know our true name."[2]

Merton sought relentlessly for the deepest self, not to be garnered by himself from the cultural fantasies of his time, nor even from roles encouraged by religious structures, but the identity revealed in the dark night of faith where the soul, stripped of certainties, encounters God. His search for the self, grounded in God, is recorded meticulously from his first writings to his last. In his early novel, *My Argument with the Gestapo*, he says: "If you want to identify me, ask me not where I live, or what I like to eat, or how I comb my hair, but ask me what I am living for, in detail, ask me what I think is keeping me from living fully for the thing I want to live for. Between the two answers you can determine the identity of any person. The better answer he has, the more of a person he is."[3] He was looking for the person God wanted him to be, hidden in Christ, and as the protagonist of the novel says, "While I'm waiting for news to guide me, I write down everything I know."

Some are scandalized that at the end of his life he seemed still to be searching (isn't a saint someone who has certitude?). I take it as a witness to his belief in the Paschal Mystery that even in his fifties, the youth of old age, he was willing to let the old Thomas Merton die once more to be born again on a distant shore.

I write of Merton not only because his life seems to suggest that we might need to question if the category "sanctity" has itself become a fossilized one that encourages the very worst sorts of imitation, but also because my own life and those of so many that I meet have been radically altered by their encounters with Merton's writings.

━━ ━━ ━━ ━━ ━━ ━━ ━━ ━━ ━━ ━━ ━━

In my sophomore year in high school, 1948, Merton's autobiography, *The Seven Storey Mountain*, was published. After devouring it, I determined that nothing else would satisfy me but religious life. In the novitiate, during my late teens and twenties, I read and reread his *Sign of Jonas*, *Seeds of Contemplation*, and *Bread in the Wilderness*. As my involvement in apostolic ministries changed me, through the fifties and sixties, I found that Merton's books grew along with me: *Conjectures of a Guilty Bystander* spoke to profound spiritual and social concerns. I heard the rumors of his dissatisfaction with religious structures, and I understood this all too clearly.

Merton's death came as a private, personal loss. I was deeply moved by the description of his funeral by a nun who had been privileged to be there. Forty friends assembled from all over the United States to await his body for eight hours, delayed in flight. The amazing diversity of these people, their ardent love for the dead monk, the deep communion of sorrow and love and thanksgiving they celebrated at the funeral mass—I thrilled to this description and to the fact that he had had a premonition of an early death and had left details of what and who he wanted at his funeral. He died the monk he had defined as "a marginal person who withdraws deliberately to the margin of society with a view to deepening fundamental human existence. . . . The marginal person, the monk, the displaced person . . . all these people live in the presence of death, which calls into question the meaning of life" (*AJ*, 305).

When I heard that he had written fifteen thousand letters, I berated myself for never having written him. I was desperate for a spiritual director in a time when the meaning of life was deeply questioned. Inspired by Ira Progoff's method of dialoguing with inner wisdom figures, for several years I made Merton my spiritual director and was much consoled by what he said. I put his picture on the wall of my room, where it has greeted me every morning since. I taught his *Contemplative Prayer* to our novices; I taught courses about him at the College of Marin; I took tapes of talks he had given to his novices with me on private retreat; I gave weekend retreats on his life and work at an ecumenical retreat center in northern California. The response to Merton never fails to surprise me, and I have met many who call themselves Merton's "children." When the sterility involved in being celibate tends to overwhelm, I am drawn to write a book called *Merton's Children*. (One woman sheepishly admitted asking her mother if she hadn't lived in London in the late thirties when Merton fathered a child there.) How could so many people with such divergent backgrounds feel such a bond? An outline of his life and some of the archetypes that he lived—monk, orphan, solitary, writer, priest, prophet—reveals that, like him or not, Merton's influence will not go away.

━━ ━━ ━━ ━ ━ ━━ ━ ━ ━━ ━━ ━━

Thomas Merton was born January 31, 1915, in wartime France, of two artists—his father from New Zealand, his mother from the United States. His mother, a rather cool woman, kept detailed descriptions of the young child and sent them to relatives. He remembers sitting under a maple tree, trying to understand what she said. I am touched by her description of the three-year-old Merton listening at a stormy window saying, "Oh, oh, Monsieur le Wind, what he say?" When he was six years old, his mother died of cancer, and he recalls that he was not allowed to see or touch her, but was given a letter from her telling him goodbye.

Though his younger brother, John Paul, stayed in America, Thomas was educated at private schools in France and England near his father painter, a confirmed wanderer. When Merton was sixteen, his father died; the youth records sobbing into the blanket on the deathbed, utterly helpless. Under the guardianship of a family friend, he continued his schooling in England, falling into a somewhat dissolute life of womanizing and drinking that was to leave him with an illegitimate child, the anger of his guardian, and a ticket back to America, where he matriculated at Columbia University. He entered fully into campus life there, was briefly a card-carrying Communist, and worked in a Harlem settlement house. It was there that he was led to study St. Augustine through meeting a Hindu, where studying William Blake for his master's thesis led him to Christ, and where he was converted and baptized a Catholic.

After graduation, he taught English at a Franciscan college in New York and considered becoming a Franciscan himself, but was rejected when he revealed his past mistakes.

In 1941, when he was twenty-seven, he entered the strictest of Catholic religious orders, the Trappists, to vow himself to a life of silence and penance. He was prepared to give up writing, but his abbot wisely encouraged him to continue. As closure to his secular life, and at what was the midpoint of his biography, he wrote *The Seven Storey Mountain*, which was published and became an instant best seller, much to his surprise and that of his superiors. For the next fourteen years, his days were taken up with long hours of prayer, reading, writing, and teaching first the young professed monks and then the many novices who had entered, swelling the ranks of the monastery, inspired by his book. Some of what he wrote was poor; later, he was ashamed of some works and even of the autobiography for its simplistic separation of the sacred and secular, for its arrogance. He was much loved by his students, for he was a fine teacher, and their love opened his heart as did the many friendships he made through letters that came flooding to him. Through all these years, the friends he had made at Columbia remained constant and devoted.

To the other monks Merton was simply Father Louis, of whom about a third would come to hear the talks he was asked to give on Sundays. His abbot for most of his religious life was a man exactly his opposite, the source of some affliction for both of them. James Fox, a business major from Harvard, was business-minded, meticulous, militaristic, pietistic (signing his letters, "to Jesus through Mary with a smile"), forbidding, suspicious, and punishing. He forbade Merton to leave the monastery for any reason, and fought his efforts to enter another, more eremitical order, the Camaldolese. Merton knew that he was not an easy subject, yet he always obeyed his abbot even if he didn't like to do so, and he radically criticized the spirituality of cheese making (the monks at

Gethsemani were making a lot of cheese as one of their industries), which he thought Fox fostered.

Merton wrote comprehensively and compulsively during these years: fifty-five books, five hundred articles, hundreds of lectures, eight volumes of history, and then all those letters. Many of the letters were written in the years when he was forbidden to publish because of his outspoken criticism on civil rights issues and Vietnam, and his support of pacifism. The influential made their way to his door, among them Eldridge Cleaver, Boris Pasternak, Joan Baez, Jacques Maritain, Dorothy Day, and John Howard Griffin—a tremendous variety of types and interests. The Catholic Peace Movement began in his hermitage. My favorite image of the opposites Merton sought to bridge is the picture Griffin gives of Merton playing Bob Dylan tapes to a puzzled Jacques Maritain, asking, "Isn't this great poetry?"

Permission to give up the arduous work of novice master, and something of the burden of communal living by moving to a hermitage, was granted to Merton three years before he died. Bidding farewell to his novices, he assured them that he was not leaving because "good old Uncle Louie had finally succeeded in twisting the abbot's arm," but because the old idea that religious life should be a convoy of trucks, everyone going thirty miles an hour, in mass production was not real monasticism. He was going to the hermitage to cast his cares upon the Lord. Although they leave behind worldly cares, religious often take on other, phony cares, and he believed that in the hermitage he could better learn to get rid of the care by going through it. Only when we are not clouded with anxieties can we see that the world is transparent of God. And in the end, he was going out to the hermitage to be kissed by God, as the hermits used to say.

He gives beautiful descriptions of his life in the hermitage. One senses the centeredness, the peace, the humor, and the simplicity of Merton's days. Some inner war was over—though not all wars.

His reading was prodigious, and like St. Thomas Aquinas, he was respectful of truth wherever he found it. When he received permission from the new abbot (one of his former students) to travel to the Far East to attend a conference on monasticism, he was as eager as a child. His *Asian Journal*, published posthumously, gives wonderful details of his openness to the Far East. The photographs of his meeting with the Dalai Lama show men whose faces look remarkably alike.

Merton died from contact with a defective electric fan in the early afternoon of December 10, 1968. His body was flown home with the bodies of American youths killed in the Vietnam War, which he had so bitterly protested. Born in the First World War, having entered the monastery at the outbreak of the Second World War (three days after the Pearl Harbor bombing), and dead in another war—it is no wonder that pacifism was his fitting prophetic plea. The effects on his dead body were listed by the State Department as follows:

1. Timex watch, value $10.00
2. One pair of dark glasses, value nil
3. Two breviaries, value nil
4. One broken rosary, value nil
5. One wooden ikon, value nil

Value of his goods: nil, nil, nil, except for the watch he wore when time stopped for him. Fitting end for a monk whose vocation he described as being that of a "marginal person."

I think one reason for Merton's profound influence is the depth to which he lived the archetypes of a monk, orphan, solitary, writer, priest, and prophet—archetypes compelling for our age, which has witnessed so many displaced persons; so many orphaned by war, or orphaned by systems they no longer believe in; so many deceived by the written and spoken word, unable to articulate and trust their own lives, unable to connect any longer to the written word of God in scripture; so many abused or deceived by religious thought or ritual, unable to find priestly people and structures to help them know they were created by a loving God; and so many outraged by abuses of power, needing a prophet to tell even in high places how God feels about injustice, how he feels, now, about the very future of the planet.

There are other archetypes that Merton lived: student (he studied and read deeply all his life), teacher, friend, and lover; but I leave the exploration of these roles to others.

Monk, orphan, solitary: I group these under one heading. The person who is called to suffer isolation, to embrace it, despite the fact that the first word spoken by God about man in the story of Genesis was, "It is not good for man to be alone." In each of the first three decades of his life, Merton lost a member of his immediate family by tragic and untimely death: at six, his mother; at sixteen, his father; and at twenty-eight, his only brother, shot down in an English warplane. The poem he wrote to his brother on the afternoon he received that news, "For My Brother: Reported Missing in Action, 1943," is one of the loveliest Merton ever wrote, containing a deep love, a profound theology of the Communion of Saints, and a belief in the efficacy of Christ's death to heal all our deadly disconnections. It ends, "The silence of Whose tears shall fall / Like bells upon your alien tomb. / Hear them and come: they call you home."

Notice the last word, "home." It is only in Christ's silent tears that one is called home. Only in the monastery did Merton find the stability so lacking in his early life; but even there he came to feel alien, not one of the convoy system, not totally at home with what he was expected to be. The contemplative has not fiery visions, but is he who has risked his mind in the desert beyond ideas where God is encountered, and in the nakedness of pure trust.

It is in solitude and aloneness that the masks and illusions we wear in order to buy love and respect soon crumble and we are confronted with the nothing from which we were made, and we either despair in self-hatred and anger or we turn ourselves over to the Father, who can from chaos bring forth life.

Merton knew well the terrifying emptiness that can come from solitude that relentlessly confronts us with our false self. He writes poignantly: "[The false self] is the man I want myself to be but who cannot exist because God does not know anything about him. And to be unknown to God is altogether too much privacy. My false and private life is the one who wants to exist outside the reach of God's will and God's love—outside of reality and outside of life. And such a self cannot help but be an illusion" (*NSC*, 34).

Merton thought that "a person is a person insofar as he has a secret, a solitude of his own that cannot be communicated to anyone else" (*NMI*, 244). Merton challenges each of us to have the courage to embrace the loneliness and alienation we experience, no matter what the nature of our bonds to others. By his life, he encourages us to make a part of our lives that solitude without which we cannot encounter the self that God intended us to be, that solitude where Christ may find us to teach what he learned in his temptations in the desert. It isn't that Christ cannot be found in the marketplace; it is that something of us cannot be found when we are in a crowd.

The second archetype he lived, excessively and even compulsively, was that of a writer. He says about himself, "Writing is a moral matter and my typewriter is an essential factor in my asceticism" (*SOJ*, 40).

His approach was as a questioner, not selling answers as ready-made cheeses: personal, informal, tentative, singular, existential, and poetic. The range of his writing was astounding: history, biography, theology, a novel, poetry, a play, literary criticism, and hagiography. There are passages of unparalleled beauty and clarity scattered throughout his works. He was what Ernest Becker calls an "erotic" thinker—one who is seeking to connect opposites, who circles about his materials, who somehow manages to leap from the page and touch deeply the reader in what he himself described as a "blaze of recognition." He used his writing as a tool in his search for God:

> If I am to be a saint—and there is nothing else that I can think of desiring to be—it seems that I must get there by writing books in a Trappist monastery. If I am to be a saint, I have not only to be a monk, which is what all monks must do to become saints, but I must also put down on paper what I have become. It may sound simple, but it is not an easy vocation. To be as good a monk as I can, and to remain myself, and to write about it: to put myself down on paper, in such a situation, with the most complete simplicity and integrity, masking nothing, confusing no issues: this is very hard, because I am all mixed up in allusions and attachments. These, too, will have to be put down. (*SOJ*, 233–34)

What a challenge he is to us to be honest about our lives, to seek to tell the truth, to be willing to write down all we think and feel so that we can better sift the wheat from the chaff. To write is both nature and work. Merton's simplicity in telling out loud his own story through his journals manifests a profound courage and faith that God is revealing himself in our lives as he has revealed himself also in the great stories of biblical revelation. His Son is his Logos: his Word made flesh. As we attempt to speak the Word, the logos of God which has never been said before we existed, we are purified and conformed to God's word that is Christ, living our lives as truly as he lived his. Others can do my work, my role;

only I can be me, the word God spoke from his creative mouth when I was conceived.

Merton also lived the archetype priest, and in a very deep way. His ordination on the Feast of the Ascension, May 26, 1949, was the happiest day of his life. It was as a priest that he craved for souls, willed to be part of the process that consumes and is sacrificed for others. He wrote of the priesthood: "More than anything else, more than ever before I beg You, my God, to kindle in my heart the love of Christ and teach me how to give myself to You in union with His Sacrifice. It will not be the first time I have reflected on the marvelous prayer the priest says when mingling a drop of water with the wine in the chalice. But I want that prayer to symbolize all that I live for" (*SOJ*, 27).

From daily crying to God and holding him in his hands, Merton learned the uncertainty of words before that powerful ritual; he learned to take his own confused, small meaning and suffering and to unite them to a greater world. From that security, he learned not to demand that everything be secure, or make perfect sense.

Through the daily Eucharist, that is *thanksgiving*, Merton grew full of that gratefulness of heart that is the essence of all prayer. His loving descriptions of nature—the wonderful rain pouring down, selling nothing; the king snake guarding his outhouse; and the trees—were all part of his priestly act of offering all creation to God, all creation that is transparent with God, if only we will still ourselves to see it.

The loving-kindness he extended to all types of men and women seems, too, characteristic of a priestly, humble, forgiving heart. As he broke the bread of Christ's life daily, so he learned to break open the bread of his own life and feed others. If the priest is that person who stands as mediator between us and God, supporting, deepening, facilitating their interchange, Merton is priest par excellence in leading others to search for the truth and depths of God's loving presence in an age of doubt and ambiguity. His witness is all the more telling because he never denied that doubt and ambiguity plagued him, too; he denied that it was an obstacle to seeking and loving God.

The beauty of Merton's priesthood shines from its simplicity, understatedness, pervasiveness, and depth. It was a Catholic priesthood, so catholic that it encompassed and mediated for the non-Catholic, too. Hard thing, that. Merton calls us by his priesthood to live the heart of the Eucharist in our own lives, to seek a sanctity in which we are sacrificed, consumed, and transformed. His willingness to let the old Merton die and be transformed indicates that he had learned not only to speak the words of transubstantiation.

If as priest Merton was deeply conservative in the most traditional sense, as prophet he was an irritant and rebel to the institutions of state, monastery, and church that had formed and nourished him. What is a prophet? One who witnesses to the fatherhood of God by expressing God's feelings. He is one seized by God to speak of his outrage against the corruption of power. The prophet is not domesticated but carries credentials of resistance—not just against the king and the people, but even against God. The prophet is one who speaks God's name with his own life, who stands in the breach, who says, "Here I am. Send me." By his "I am," the prophet witnesses to Yahweh: *I am Who I Am.* The prophet must speak, whether what he says pleases or not.

Merton spoke out about social justice, about war and civil rights, so clearly that he was silenced. He obeyed and continued to mimeograph letters. How could a monk know about these issues, locked away as he was in a monastery, his critics would chide. How could a monk *not,* if he had rightly understood the contemplative life and prayed it, was Merton's response. He wrote: "Creativity has to begin with me and I cannot sit here wasting time urging the monastic institution to become creative and prophetic. . . . What each one of us has to do, what I have to do, is to buckle down and really start investigating new possibilities in our own lives; and if new possibilities mean radical changes, all right" (*CWA*, 222). Relentlessly, ceaselessly, Merton spoke and wrote the truth as he thought God willed.

How willing are we to acknowledge our feelings and speak them out—much less try to imagine how God sees the evils threatening to destroy the world? Perhaps it was the discipline of recording his feelings that purified Merton and enabled him to listen to that other inner voice commanding him to take as his own the concerns of a larger life and world. Though he was a connoisseur of his own solitary self and knew it well, Merton reached out to the other who was his brother, his sister, wherever in loneliness and solitude they were overlooked. From the consciousness of his own personal sinfulness as a child of nine, shutting out his younger brother John Paul who wanted to play with the gang, Merton connected to a consciousness of social sin—how we shut out the minority, the stranger.

Brother, father, friend Thomas Merton, how much courage you give me by your honesty; by your fidelity to your commitments, no matter what the cost; by your humor and grace; by your breadth and depth; and by your eccentricities and doubts, the chills that arose from your depths. You were faithful to your God, your friends, and yourself. You who sought sanctity through separation from the world when young, sought sanctity through full humanness as you grew older—like your Master not clinging to power, but emptying yourself to feel and live and witness that the vulnerability and darkness of the fully human is God's workplace, where he molds men and women fit to preach the Good News.

Merton, you are "good news" indeed. You take the stuffiness from holiness, the abstract pietism from prayer, the dogmatism from dogma, and the faithlessness from the dark night of faith.

Brother Merton, mystic, help us to master the darkness encountered from the pilgrimage within and the darkness of enchainment to the world without. For, as the Hindu scriptures say, "Dark is the night for him who thinks that the world without is all that counts. Darker still the night for him who thinks that the world within is all that counts." Help us not to fear the dark.

Father Merton, give us the courage of your prophetic vision that knew how to revolt with an action, a word steeped in prayer. For you lived and loved that quotation of Georges Bernanos: "Angers, daughters of despair, creep and twist like worms. Prayer is, all things considered, the only form of revolt that stays standing up" (*CGB*, 162).

FOR PERSONAL REFLECTION

1. What you are living for? What is keeping you from living fully for the thing you want to live for?
2. Do you feel that the notion of sanctity has become institutionalized? Do you have the same idea of sanctity you had when you were younger?
3. In what ways has Merton influenced your life?
4. Who and what would you like at your funeral?
5. When have you felt most orphaned? Solitary? Do you make time in your life for solitude?
6. What contrasts of Merton's are particularly appealing to you? Particularly distasteful?
7. When have you been drawn to writing as a tool to find God? What blocks you from writing as prayer?
8. What writers have brought you nearer to yourself and God because they wrote of their lives?
9. What priests have mediated God for you?
10. When have you felt called to protest some injustice?
11. Compose a prayer to Merton, or a dialogue touching those areas of your life where you feel comforted or challenged by him.

3.

On Spiritual
Exploration

Robert Ellsberg

Over a hundred years have passed since Thomas Merton's birth in 1915, and fifty years since his death in 1968. Yet his story and his writings continue to attract a wide audience, sustained not only by the astonishing number of books he published during his life but also by the continuous stream of volumes, biographies, and critical studies published since his death.

What accounts for this enduring interest? Merton was a poet and artist; a born rebel who spent most of his life under a vow of obedience; a man thoroughly formed by the tempestuous currents of the twentieth century who found peace and meaning in an austere brand of monasticism rooted in the twelfth century; a Catholic priest who entered into creative dialogue with people of all faiths, especially the religions of the East; and a man whose solitude became a watchtower, allowing him to discern with uncommon insight the pathologies of our time. He was a man of the widest

vision who wished to reach beyond the confines of his solitary life
to enter into dialogue with writers, artists, activists, and visionaries
of all traditions.

He was all these things, but for many who have been fascinated
and inspired by his work, Merton was the consummate spiritual
explorer—one who never ceased in the quest to know God and
to know himself, to grow in the direction of a truth beyond words
and images, and to report back on what he had discovered. For
spiritual explorers like Merton, their message is ultimately rooted
in their own inner journey. And for many spiritual seekers of the
past fifty years, an encounter with Thomas Merton has been a
significant milestone on their own journey.

Merton first came to the attention of the world in 1948 with
the publication of his autobiography, *The Seven Storey Mountain*.
It told the story—by turns funny and sad—of his orphaned childhood, his efforts as a true man of his age to "ransack and rob the
world of all its pleasures and satisfactions," and of the intimations
of something deeper, which led him first to the Catholic Church
and ultimately to the Trappist Abbey of Gethsemani in Kentucky.
On a retreat there, he felt he had found his true home at last. "This
is the center of America," he wrote. "It is an axle around which
the whole country blindly turns" (*SJ*, 183). Admitted as a novice
on December 10, 1941, just days after Pearl Harbor, he sought a
life of prayer and penance. He desired to "give everything," and
so, as he wrote, "Brother Matthew locked the gate behind me and
I was enclosed in the four walls of my new freedom" (*SSM*, 410).

In entering the monastery, Merton felt not only that he was
leaving the world and giving up "everything," but also that he was
leaving behind a certain "Thomas Merton" with all his anxious
desire to be somebody, his demanding ego, and his tendency to sar-
casm and scorn for people who didn't meet his standards. With the
anonymous monks in their white habits, he intended to drown to
the world, to be invisible, a nobody. . . . It didn't quite go that way.

With the astonishing success of *The Seven Storey Mountain*, Merton was suddenly the most famous monk in America. The irony was not lost on him. And yet his superiors believed his writing had something to offer the world, and they ordered him to keep at it. And so he did. Yet for all the books he would go on to produce, in the public mind he was eternally fixed at the point where his memoir ended—as a young monk with his cowl pulled over his head, happily convinced that in joining an austere medieval community he had fled the modern world, never to return. It was difficult for readers to appreciate that this picture represented only the beginning of Merton's journey as a monk.

At least Merton himself had intuited that there was more to come. His memoir ended with a Latin motto: *Sit finis libri; non finis quarendi* (Here ends the book, but not the searching). In ways he probably couldn't have imagined, this proved to be literally true. Over the next twenty years, Merton continued to search and grow more deeply into his vocation and his relationship with Christ. Eventually he reached the point where he would write, with some exasperation, "*The Seven Storey Mountain* is the work of a man I never even heard of" (*ES* 458). And at that point he still had a long way to go!

One aspect of the book that he particularly came to regret was the attitude of pious scorn directed at "the world" and its unfortunate citizens. He had seemed to regard the monastery as a secluded haven set apart from "the news and desires and appetites and conflicts" that bedeviled ordinary humanity.

In 1948, the year of *Seven Storey Mountain*, an errand into Louisville occasioned one of his first trips outside the monastery. In his journal, he noted piously: "Going into Louisville the other day, I wasn't struck by anything in particular. Although I felt completely alienated from everything in the world and all its activity." Though he felt the people were "worthy of sympathizing with," overall he judged the excursion "boring."[1]

What a difference a decade would make! In 1958 he recorded in his journals the radically different impact of another errand into Louisville. "On the corner of Fourth and Walnut in the center of the shopping district"—an intersection that has recently been rechristened Thomas Merton Plaza—he experienced a moment of mystical awareness that inspired one of the most famous passages in all his books: "I was suddenly overwhelmed with the realization that I loved all those people, that they were mine and I theirs, that we could not be alien to one another even though we were total strangers. It was like waking from a dream of separateness, of spurious self-isolation in a special world, the world of renunciation and supposed holiness" (*CGB*, 155).

In that dream of separateness, he is describing an understanding of holiness that had animated his early life as a monk, that is, an understanding of holiness primarily defined by ascetical self-denial. In its place comes an understanding of holiness based on compassionate solidarity with his fellow human beings. And Merton came to see that the entire purpose of the monastic life, or any spiritual search for that matter, was to achieve this vision, this awakening from a dream of separateness to realize our underlying oneness, our unity in what he called "a hidden wholeness."

No doubt this marked a crucial turning point in his evolution as a monk. For years, Merton had devoted creative thought to the meaning of monastic and contemplative life. But from this point on, he became increasingly concerned with making connections between the monastery and the wider world. His writing assumed a more ecumenical and compassionate tone. Reading his old writing, he observed: "I cannot go back to the earlier fervor or the asceticism that accompanied it. The new fervor will be rooted not in asceticism but in humanism" (*SFS*, 237). For Merton it was a kind of rebirth. "I am finally coming out of the chrysalis," he wrote. "Now the pain and struggle of fighting my way out into something new and much bigger. I must see and embrace God in the whole world."[2]

This increasing openness was also reflected in his writings on holiness. Previously, in thrall to a dream of separateness and "supposed holiness," he had held up the monastery as an ideal arena for achieving sanctity. Now he maintained that being a saint was simply a matter of consenting to God's creative love. "The pale flowers of the dogwood outside this window are saints," he wrote. "The lakes hidden among the hills are saints, and the sea too is a saint who praises God without interruption in her majestic dance" (*NSC*, 30).

And what about human beings, for whom the problem of sanctity is a little more complicated? "For me sanctity consists in being myself," he wrote. "For me to be saint means to be myself. Therefore the problem of sanctity and salvation is in fact the problem of finding out who I am and of discovering my true self" (*NSC*, 31).

Another way of putting this would be in terms of abandoning the false self, the mask we present to the world and to ourselves. The whole journey of Thomas Merton to this point could be seen as putting off a series of masks—the bad boy, the sophisticated twentieth-century man, the good Catholic, the perfect monk—to become his true self, the saint that God created him to be. But it was the same challenge for everyone. The path to sanctity for Thomas Merton the monk was not really so very different from the path of every other person in the world.

Suddenly Merton began reaching out to an ever-widening circle of correspondents: Russian novelists, Zen masters, beat poets, intellectuals, and peace activists. Along with his writings on prayer and spirituality, he began to produce prophetic essays on the issues of the day, particularly the Cold War atmosphere of fear and the threat of nuclear war. In the first of many articles published in the *Catholic Worker*, he wrote: "Peace is to be preached, nonviolence is to be explained as a practical method, and not left to be mocked as an outlet for crackpots, who want to make a show of themselves. . . . It is the great Christian task of our time. Everything else is secondary, for the survival of the human race depends on it."[3]

All of these social issues, he believed, including racism and a growing concern for ecology, were ultimately spiritual questions. They were rooted in a distorted spiritual vision in which we failed to recognize our underlying oneness. This was the vision that underlay his mystical epiphany at Fourth and Walnut. Referring to the people he saw on the street, he had written: "If only they could all see themselves as they really *are*. If only we could see each other that way all the time. There would be no more war, no more hatred, no more cruelty, no more greed" (*CGB*, 155).

In reflections on the mentality of Adolf Eichmann, one of the architects of the Holocaust, he was struck by the determination of psychiatrists who examined him that Eichmann was totally sane.[4] We were living in a time when perfectly sane men, following the dictates of reason and logic, were capable of engineering the destruction of the earth. In such a time, what was needed were men and women of imagination—poets, rebels, prophets, and yes, monks—who could pierce the shell of functional logic to act on the basis of a deeper spiritual wisdom, and share that vision with others.

Not everyone, to be sure, was happy with this new Thomas Merton. They preferred "the official voice of Trappist silence, the monk with his hood up and his back to the camera, brooding over the waters of an artificial lake," as Merton himself described the old, stereotyped him. The new Merton, he went on, was "not the petulant and uncanonizable modern Jerome who never got over the fact that he could give up beer." To this, he added words intended to shock his pious devotees: "(I drink beer whenever I can lay my hands on any. I love beer, and by that very act, the world.") (*CWA*, 142).

And yet he believed his love for the world implied a prophetic stance, a need to criticize its spiritual delusions and, in collaboration with like-minded spiritual seekers, "to make the world better, more free, more just, more livable, more human." In a preface to the Japanese edition of *Seven Storey Mountain*, he put it more specifically:

> It is my intention to make my entire life a rejection of, a protest against the crimes and injustices of war and political tyranny which threaten to destroy the whole race of man and world with him. By my monastic life and vows I am saying NO to all the concentration camps, the aerial bombardments, the staged political trials, the judicial murders, the racial injustices, the economic tyrannies, and the whole socio-economic apparatus which seems geared for nothing but global destruction. . . . If I say NO to all these secular forces, I also say YES to all that is good in the world and in man. I say YES to all that is beautiful in nature.[5]

While some of Merton's readers wished he would stick with the old writing on the liturgy and prayer, there were also many new friends who wondered what he was doing holed up in a monastery; wasn't this life of prayer and solitude a cop-out from the more relevant action in the streets? For Merton, this line of thought never posed a serious temptation. In fact, his increasing engagement with the world outside the monastery was accompanied by a deeper call to solitude.

Monks in the Benedictine tradition, including Trappists, take a vow of "stability." In a literal sense, this is a vow to remain in the monastery to which they are attached. It is a commitment not to run away when things get tough, or to imagine that life will be easier if you just don't have to put up with all the idiots around you. But there is a deeper principle involved than just staying put. Complementing the vow of stability is a second Benedictine principle called *conversatio morum*—literally "the conversion of manners." Essentially it refers to the ongoing process of growth and spiritual maturity, going deeper into the heart of your vocation. The task of becoming a monk doesn't end when you take your vows; it is an ongoing journey that lasts a lifetime.

There is no doubt that for Merton the vow of stability was a particular challenge. In his early book *The Sign of Jonas*, he described stability as the belly of the whale, the mysterious paradox through which, like the prophet Jonah, he was being carried to his ultimate destination (*SOJ*, epigraph).

Though his early monastic writings describe a feeling of giddy homecoming, his later journals tell a different story: irritation with the banal business operations of the monastery; conflicts with his abbot; and frustration with a religious system that seemed determined to stifle his yearnings for a life of solitary prayer.

In his early years, Merton was beset by the notion of joining a "purer" order, the Carthusians or the Camaldolese. This later gave way to fantasies of fleeing to a hermitage or a community in Mexico, Nicaragua, Chile, the Southwest, or Alaska—seemingly anywhere but Gethsemani. Inevitably these plans were quashed by his superiors, if they had not already been replaced by newer schemes. In light of such frustrations he could write: "I think the monastic life as we live it here warps people. Kills their spirit, reduces them to something less than human" (*SFS*, 285). He proclaims to his journal: "It is intolerable to have to spend my life contributing to the maintenance of this illusion. The illusion of the great, gay, joyous, peppy, optimistic, Jesus-loving, one hundred percent American Trappist monastery" (*SFS*, 290).

Eventually, Merton realized that he didn't need to leave Gethsemani. What he really wanted was greater interior space to define the meaning of his contemplative vocation. It was a call not to leave the monastery but to rediscover its inner meaning: "It does not much matter where you are, as long as you can be at peace about it and live your life. The place certainly will not live my life for me. I have to live it for myself" (*SFS*, 236). Where would he find the solitude he sought? "Here or there makes no difference. Somewhere, nowhere, beyond all 'where.' Solitude outside geography, or in it. No matter" (*SFS*, 359).

At this point, after years of clamoring for a more solitary life, Merton was given permission to live in a simple hermitage on the monastery grounds, a situation that proved conducive to both prayer and creative work. Happily, he wrote, "The sense of a journey ended, of wandering at an end. *The first time in my life I ever really felt that I had come home and that my roaming and looking were ended*" (*TTW*, 79–80).

In the pure silence and solitude of his hermitage, Merton felt he was making his own kind of protest against a world in which communication had been replaced by party platforms and advertising slogans; in which time and even existence itself were measured out and weighed for their productive value. As a spiritual explorer, he felt a special connection with the Desert Fathers of the fourth century, who had left the comforts and compromises of a supposedly Christian world for the solitude of the wilderness. In words that really applied to himself, he wrote:

> What the [Desert] Fathers sought most of all was their own true self, in Christ. And in order to do this, they had to reject completely the false, formal self, fabricated under social compulsion in "the world." They sought a way to God that was uncharted and freely chosen, not inherited from others who had mapped it out beforehand. They sought a God whom they alone could find, not one who was "given" in a set, stereotyped form by somebody else. . . . We need to learn from these men of the fourth century how to ignore prejudice, defy compulsion and strike out fearlessly into the unknown. (*WD*, 5–6)

Merton himself, of course, was seeking a "way to God that was uncharted and freely chosen, not inherited from others who had mapped it out beforehand."

There are risks to be faced by those who travel without maps. The solitary desert explorers whom Merton admired faced many perils in the form of demons and other temptations. The same was true for Merton. It was soon after settling into his hermitage that he faced his own final and most difficult temptation: falling in love and conducting a secret affair with a nurse he met in a hospital in Louisville.

This episode, which lasted over a period of several months, is described in great detail in volume six of his published journals. The story is too complex to summarize adequately here. [See Kaya Oakes's essay.—Ed.] Suffice to say that in this affair Merton experienced a liberating sense of his capacity to love and receive love. His journal is at times deeply moving, heartbreaking, and also exasperating. Some have romanticized the episode, feeling that he should—as one of his poet friends put it—"follow the ecstasy" right out of the monastery. That was a serious option. But what was not an option was to have it both ways—to suppose that there was some way to be both a hermit and a lover. What was at stake was not simply the violation of his monastic vows, but the danger of a kind of doubleness and lack of integrity. "What do I fear most?" he wrote. "Forgetting and ignorance of the inmost truth of my being. To forget who I am, to be lost in what I am not, to fail my own inner truth, to get carried away in what is not true to me" (*LL*, 332).

When he was honest with himself, Merton realized that he was ultimately wedded to his vocation to solitude. Regarding his vows, he wrote, "I cannot be true to myself if I am not true to so deep a commitment" (*LL*, 162). He came to the conclusion that his vocation was not just for himself, but that it meant something to the rest of the world.

In effect, he returned to the idea that had first attracted him to the abbey—that the monastery was in some sense the *axis mundi*, that the monks were in some way, with their prayers and their faithfulness, keeping the world turning. But now he was understanding faithfulness not just in terms of an outward form, or a particular setting, but in terms of the deepest core of himself. The difference suggested that this was not some special vocation for Trappist monks. Wherever people were faithful to their true selves, they were the *axis mundi* standing up for peace, against lies, in the integrity of their witness, in creating something beautiful and true, in their loving service of their neighbors. . . . For some this might be in a soup kitchen, a studio, a marriage, or a prison cell. For him, it was in his hermitage.

On September 10, 1966, he signed a short formula in which he committed himself "to live in solitude for the rest of my life" (*LL*, 129). He continued to be carried toward his destiny in the belly of a paradox, traveling without maps, stumbling in the dark, but trusting that he was being guided toward his true home.

In 1968, the last year of his life, a more flexible abbot permitted Merton at last to venture forth. He accepted an invitation to address an international conference of Christian monks in Bangkok. Merton was particularly excited about the prospect of exploring his deep interest in Eastern spirituality. In this respect, as his journals show, the trip marked a new breakthrough, another wider encounter with the "gate of heaven" that is everywhere. He met with Buddhist and Hindu monks. In India he had several significant meetings with the Dalai Lama.

In Ceylon, one week before his death, in the presence of the enormous statues of the reclining Buddha, he was "suddenly, almost forcibly, jerked clean out of the habitual, half-tied vision of things, and an inner clearness, clarity, as if exploding from the rocks themselves, became evident and obvious . . . everything is emptiness and everything is compassion" (*OSM*, 323). It was the culmination of his Asian pilgrimage: "I mean, I know and have seen what I was obscurely looking for" (*OSM*, 323). And perhaps it was something more.

On December 10, 1968, he delivered his talk in Bangkok and afterward retired to his room for a shower and nap. In this talk, in the last hour of his life, he spoke of the monastic principle of *conversatio morum*—what he called the most mysterious and yet most essential of all monastic vows. He interpreted it as "a commitment to total inner transformation of one sort or another—a commitment to become a completely new man. It seems to me that that could be regarded as the end of the monastic life, and that no matter where one attempts to do this, that remains the essential thing" (*AJ*, 337).

A short while after delivering this talk, Merton was found dead in his room, apparently electrocuted by the faulty wiring of a fan.

I am among the countless number whose lives were changed by the encounter with Thomas Merton. I first read him when I was in high school and discovered, among other things, that there was room in Christianity for engagement with Gandhi, Zen Buddhism, the war in Vietnam, and a general spirit of mischief that appealed to my teenaged sensibility. Later, I read *The Seven Storey Mountain*, made a retreat at Gethsemani, and decided to become a Catholic. I give credit to Merton for inspiring my work over many years in telling the stories of saints and holy people. From him, I learned that saints are more than the otherworldly heroes of pious legend—close to God but not exactly human.

In fact, as Merton observed, sanctity is really a matter of being more fully human: "This implies a greater capacity for concern, for suffering, for understanding, for sympathy, also for humor, for joy, for appreciation for the good and beautiful things of life."[6] Certainly those words could serve as an apt description of the man himself.

I also came to see that becoming a saint is not a matter of conforming oneself to some cookie-cutter image of sanctity. It is a process—one that is never really finished, the work of a lifetime. Essentially this is the meaning Merton attached to the vow of *conversatio morum*: a matter of going deeper, continuously turning toward God, or as St. Paul it, putting off the old person and putting on Christ. As a result of this process, we do not emerge as another Thomas Merton or any other saint. In fact, as Merton would ultimately reflect, "For me to be a saint means to be myself" (*NSC*, 31).

So what are the odds that Merton himself might be canonized and named an official saint? Slim, I would say. The Church prefers its saints to fit into a more conventional mold of sanctity. Merton, for all his obedient submission to authority over many years, still makes some people nervous. Though totally rooted in his Catholic faith and his priesthood, he was constantly causing headaches for his superiors and seemed always straining to burst through neat, official boundaries, resisting efforts to pin him down, box him in, or use him as a poster boy for any cause or institution. Maybe this makes sense. As he wrote, perhaps with a dose of self-justification: "One of the first signs of a saint may well be the fact that other people do not know what to make of him. In fact they are not sure whether he is crazy or only proud. . . . He cannot seem to make his life fit in with the books" (*NSC*, 103).

And yet in 2015, in his speech before the United States Congress, Pope Francis singled out Merton as one of "four great Americans," specifically commending his capacity to think outside the box. Merton, he said, "was above all a man of prayer, a thinker who challenged the certitudes of his time and opened new horizons for souls and for the Church. He was also a man of dialogue, a promoter of peace between peoples and religions."[7] So who can say? In living out a model of holiness not easily pigeonholed in a Catholic mold, Merton represented a type of holiness particularly suited and necessary to our times. Responding to God's call, he let go of his possessions, his ego, even a spurious kind of "supposed holiness"—until he came to rest in God's emptiness and compassion.

As a spiritual explorer, traveling without maps, Merton created his path by walking it. In his own struggles to be faithful, he created possibilities for many others to live with greater compassion, courage, and integrity in our frantic and imperiled century. Through his writings, he cast seeds of contemplation and communion that continue to bear fruit in diverse and unexpected places. For those of us who struggle to see the road before us, he is a welcome companion.

4.

How to Be a Friend

Gregory K. Hillis

For, you see, when "‾" enter into a dialogue with "you"
and each of us knows who is speaking, it turns out that
we are both Christ.
> —Thomas Merton, letter to John Harris,
> January 31, 1959 (*HGL*, 387)

In 1961, Jim Forest watched Thomas Merton write a letter. A
prominent peace activist who was himself the recipient of more
than seventy of the monk's letters, Forest was at the Abbey of Gethsemani, meeting Merton for the first time. During the course of
their meeting, Forest gave Merton a letter that a fellow volunteer at
the Catholic Worker had asked him to deliver. The letter was critical of Merton, expressing admiration for his antiwar writings, but
adding dismay that he would stay in a monastery when he could
instead be active in the world for the cause of peace. What fascinated Forest wasn't so much the letter itself or Merton's response
to it; it was the experience of watching Merton.

He had a small office just outside the novitiate classroom. On his desk was a large grey Royal typewriter.
He inserted a piece of monastery stationary and wrote
a reply at what seemed to me the speed of light. I had
never seen anyone write so quickly. You might sometimes see a skilled stenographer type at such speed
when copying a text, but even in a city newsroom of
that period one rarely saw anyone writing at a similar
pace. The sheet of paper was in danger of bursting
into flame.[1]

Forest recalls that in just a few minutes, Merton was able to compose a well-written and carefully reasoned letter that filled one
single-spaced sheet of paper.

There are two things worth noting about Forest's story. First,
and this is characteristic, Merton did not dismiss the correspondent
out of hand, but took him and his concerns seriously enough to
write an immediate response. Second, the story goes some way
toward explaining how Merton was able to write so many letters
during his lifetime. The Thomas Merton Center at Bellarmine University, the official repository for Merton's literary estate, currently
has in its archives 15,000 pieces of correspondence to over 2,100
individuals. Five volumes of selected letters have been published
thus far, each volume organized along a different theme in Merton's
life and thought, and the publishing of Merton's correspondence
with particular individuals, including Robert Giroux and Rosemary Radford Ruether, continues.[2] Yet thousands of Merton's
letters remain unpublished, and more come to light each year. As
the editors of a collection of Merton's most important letters write,
"Thomas Merton was one of the most prolific and provocative
letter writers of the twentieth century" (LIL, vii).

All of this correspondence is surprising given that Merton was
a monk in a contemplative monastery who continually expressed
longing for greater solitude, arguing that community life, at
least as practiced at Gethsemani, did not lend itself to the life of

contemplation for which he yearned. Why would a monk desiring solitude carry on such a massive correspondence? Here is one of the paradoxes of Merton's life. He could not live without solitude. He also could not live without his friends, some of whom he knew personally, some of whom he knew only through letters. The volume and content of his letters indicate that he thrived on his connections with those outside the monastery. The friendships he maintained through his letters enabled him to understand more thoroughly what was going on in the world and to enter into dialogue with a diverse group of people. Just as importantly, these friendships gave him life. In a letter to Pope John XXIII, Merton described his correspondence as "an apostolate of friendship," suggesting that he viewed his letters as a ministry to others (*HGL*, 104). However, it becomes clear that Merton carried on his correspondence not just for the benefit of others. He needed those friendships just as much as others needed him.

My goal here is to examine what the letters tell us about Merton the friend and, in particular, how Merton's humility manifested itself in his correspondence with friends and played a pivotal role in developing and sustaining those friendships through the years. His humility translated into a radical openness whereby he took his correspondents seriously and gave himself fully to them in the best way he knew how—through words. The result is that Merton, a cloistered monk, developed friendships of remarkable intimacy with those outside the cloister, even with those he never met in person. I will trace how his humility shines through his letters.

HUMILITY IN SELF-REVELATION

In *New Seeds of Contemplation*, Merton writes about the true and the false self, arguing that we are tempted constantly toward unreality; that is, we are tempted not to exist as we really are but to construct "selves" or "masks" that prevent us and others from seeing ourselves in our reality. He writes, "We may wear now one mask and now another, and never, if we so desire, appear with our own true face" (*NSC*, 32). Merton's letters reveal a man unmasked, someone who manifests to his correspondents not only that he wants to get to know them beyond their masks but also that he is open to being known as he really is. Knowing that letters were the primary way he established and maintained friendships, Merton held little back when corresponding, revealing his thoughts and fears, and reflecting on his own self. We see this even in the circular letters that he occasionally sent to friends. His correspondence frequently became unmanageable, given the volume, and knowing that he owed responses to letters he had received, and that he could not possibly write personally to everyone, Merton wrote circular letters that were mimeographed and sent. What is remarkable about these circular letters is how personal Merton gets in them. There is no trace of the kind of form letters many of us receive at Christmas from friends and relatives, which usually speak only to the highlights of a year and present a portrait of ideality as if life were utter perfection. Instead, Merton writes openly and honestly about what has been going on in his life and about his work.

His circular letter from the summer of 1967 is a case in point. Merton reflects candidly about what two years in the solitude of the hermitage have taught him about his writing, and about his involvement in contemporary issues:

> I admit that I have not kept many secrets, profound or otherwise. And the risk of putting my cards on the table has been worthwhile, because I have learned from it. More and more the cards I have been putting on the table have been saying: "I don't know the answers, but I have some questions I'd like to share with you." There is always an implication that it means something to know the questions, especially if they are common questions. But now I am beginning to wonder if I even know the questions, or if they are common to others. (*RJ*, 104–5)

There is no sense in these lines that Merton wants to put himself forward as an authority, as someone who has something to say that others need to hear. Rather, he forthrightly expresses doubt about the value of his writing, wondering not only whether he has answers, but even whether the questions he asks are the ones needing to be addressed. Later in the same letter, Merton refers to the recent death of Victor Hammer, one of his best friends, and conveys his grief: "When someone like that dies, you begin to realize how a man like Camus could be so fiercely convinced that death just *should not be*. It is literally absurd that a person should cease to exist, and as Christians we believe that they do not do so. . . . Pray for him, please" (*RJ*, 105). Merton is clearly struggling with the death of his friend, and feels no need to hold back in expressing his grief. A humble honesty of self-revelation is manifested. We see a man unwilling to hide behind the veneer of perfection.

The self-revelatory nature of Merton's correspondence is also on display in his correspondence with Abdul Aziz, a Sufi Muslim in Pakistan with whom Merton exchanged letters from 1960 to 1968. These are, to my mind, some of Merton's most beautiful and profound letters. In them, Merton is completely himself, totally without pretense. He expresses his desire to learn more about Sufism from Aziz, and Aziz in turn is enthusiastic to learn more about Christian mysticism. The two exchanged books— Merton sent to Aziz his own books as well as classics of Christian mysticism, and Aziz sent Merton books about Sufism—and they exchanged ideas, each one eagerly answering and asking questions. Even more significantly, they shared with each other their experiences of prayer with such openness that Merton refers to Aziz and himself as "brothers in prayer and worship no matter what may be the doctrinal differences that separate our minds" (*HGL*, 49).

Indeed, Merton shares details about his prayer life with Aziz in a manner we find nowhere else in his writings. In December

1965, Aziz wrote two letters in which he asked Merton for details about his life at the hermitage and about his method of meditation. Merton describes what daily life was like for him, from rising at 2:30 in the morning to going to bed at 7:30 p.m., but it is his account of his method of meditation that is most interesting. After telling Aziz that he devotes approximately three hours each day to meditation, Merton describes this way of prayer in words worth quoting at length:

> Strictly speaking I have a very simple way of prayer. It is centered entirely on attention to the presence of God and to His will and His love. That is to say that it is centered on *faith* by which alone we can know the presence of God. One might say this gives my meditation the character described by the Prophet as "being before God as if you saw Him." Yet it does not mean imagining anything or conceiving a precise image of God, for to my mind this would be a kind of idolatry. On the contrary, it is a matter of adoring Him as invisible and infinitely beyond our comprehension, and realizing Him as all. My prayer tends very much toward what you call *fana*. There is in my heart this great thirst to recognize totally the nothingness of all that is not God. . . . If I am still present "myself" this I recognize as an obstacle about which I can do nothing unless He Himself removes the obstacle. (*HGL*, 63–64)

Using terminology and imagery comprehensible to his Sufi correspondent, Merton goes into intimate detail. But what is noteworthy is not simply the detail, but the fact that he describes his personal method of meditation at all. While Merton wrote volumes about prayer and the contemplative life, nowhere else in his writing does he so openly reveal his own way of prayer, preferring instead to describe the life of prayer and its fruits using broad strokes. But with his Muslim correspondent, Merton decides to put aside his reticence for the sake of their friendship. "I do not ordinarily write about such things," Merton remarks, "and I ask you therefore to be discreet about it. But I write this as a testimony of confidence and friendship" (*HGL*, 64).

HUMILITY IN ACKNOWLEDGING FAULT

Those familiar with his journals know that, particularly in the mid-1950s, Merton struggled with his vocation. He wanted more solitude and expressed dismay with the state of monastic life at Gethsemani. His letters to friends during this time often contain a litany of grievances about the monastery and the abbot, Dom James Fox, though Merton also usually acknowledges that he is not above reproach. Merton was brutally honest about his struggles and about what these struggles had to say about his state of mind and soul. A good example can be found in letters he sent to his literary agent, Naomi Burton Stone, in 1956.

In these, Merton expresses his desire for greater solitude, rather harshly referring to the "spiritual adolescence which is called the monastery of Gethsemani"(*LIL*, 68), yet he also looks with honesty at himself and shares with Stone what he sees, recognizing that he is not without fault. He tells her that he has been doing a great deal of "wrestling" with himself and acknowledges that the old Merton—the pride-filled, ambitious writer—continues to dog him, and that his wrestling has led him finally to get rid of some of that person, although he realizes that the struggle is far from over: "I do not particularly want the survival of the person and even writer I have been. Although I do have enough sense to realize that this is what I shall always probably be. But my true self is not one that has to be thought about and propped up with rationalizations. He only has to be lived, and he is lived, in Christ, under the surface of the unquiet sea in which the other one is busy drowning" (*LIL*, 69). This is a remarkable passage of honest self-reflection that manifests a monk unwilling to let pride keep him from acknowledging his faults and inner turmoil to a friend.

At the same time, Merton's complaints about the monastic life could become wearying, and a couple of months after he sent that letter, he sent another to Stone in which he again criticized life at Gethsemani. Stone had had enough of this, and told him so: "I think because you have decided that you want a certain kind of monastic life, you want the cross you choose not the one that happens to have your name on it, you dream of journeys you are not allowed to take and instead of waking up and putting the dream from your mind you wake up and write it down and mail it off to Cincinnati (or me)."[3] She asks, "How would that strike you in another, Father Master?" referring to Merton by his title as novice master, and therefore as spiritual director for incoming monks at the monastery. Stone's letter of reproach is remarkable for its forthrightness, which speaks volumes about the kinds of relationships Merton fostered through his correspondence. Stone was Merton's literary agent, but through the letters they exchanged she had become far more than that to him. Merton refers to her in one letter as a "sister" and therefore as one with whom he shared a particular intimacy (*LIL*, 68). And Stone clearly understood them to have the kind of intimate relationship that allowed her to address Merton as honestly and critically as she did.

Both their intimacy and Merton's humility are on display in his reply to her reproach. While he expresses some confusion about her letter and even defends himself, he does not put on airs. There is no sense that he, a world-famous monk and writer, was above Stone's criticisms. Rather, he takes her criticisms to heart and hastens to repair their breach of friendship with a vulnerable self-assessment. He tells her that he exaggerated many of his complaints in order to be witty and clever: "I was only rattling the bars of my crib because I thought you liked it" (*LIL*, 71). More than that, he acknowledges that she was right to call him out for his excessive complaining, confessing that he had used her as a sounding board for his frustrations without being adequately attuned to her feelings: "I am childish, I am selfish, I love to gripe. I want to complain and have someone to complain to, and for a while you were elected. I am sorry. It won't happen again, and at the same time I will make a serious effort to grow up" (*LIL*, 72). A few weeks later, he responds with a long missive in which he opens up to Stone about his spiritual life, telling her that he cannot but write to her about himself because "[y]ou are my good friend and one I can talk to, and I can't talk to most of those here as I can to you" (*LIL*, 73).

HUMILITY IN TAKING PEOPLE SERIOUSLY

In a letter to Daniel Berrigan, Merton described his correspondence as "a kind of Sisyphus act: rolling the boulder up the hill and then having it roll down again" (*LIL*, 72). This is a consistent refrain in Merton's letters, as he apologizes over and over to friends for not replying earlier to letters they have sent. However, while the sheer scale of letters Merton received was certainly part of his "Sisyphus act," another aspect of the problem was that he wanted to respond carefully and precisely to as many letters as he could. And he wanted to do so because he took each of those who wrote to him seriously, as people meriting careful consideration *as people*, regardless of who they were.

We've seen this already in the examples above, but Merton's respect for his correspondents is perhaps most evident in letters he wrote to children and teenagers. At the age of sixteen, Suzanne Butorovich wrote to Merton in 1967, asking for a contribution to her underground newspaper. She described to him various aspects of her life and offered to 'educate" him in pop music. Merton's response to her is lovely. Not only does he send her something for her newspaper, but he also treats her request with absolute seriousness by letting her know that she should feel free to publish whatever she likes from his submission, or not: "Take what you want: don't take all of this selection unless you like it all. Maybe you won't like any, but if you listen to it right you probably will" (*RJ*, 308). As for her offer to educate him about pop music, Merton is all ears, telling her that he is "a confirmed jazzman" and so could do with learning more about what she likes (*RJ*, 309). His conclusion to the letter is intimate in its playfulness, inviting further correspondence: "Keep in touch. I live in the woods and borrowed a record player. I am a real sneaky hermit and oh yes I love the hippies and am an underground hippy monk but I don't need LSD to turn on either. The birds turn me on" (*RJ*, 309).

Butorovich took his invitation to keep in touch to heart, and what emerged was a friendship that lasted until Merton's death. Merton's own intimacy was reciprocated by the teenager, who occasionally addressed her letters to "Hippie Hermit" and signed off as "The Nut" or "Disaster." They shared their thoughts on music (the Beatles come up regularly, as do Jefferson Airplane and the Grateful Dead), Kahlil Gibran, Zen Buddhism, and cooking, among other topics. She expressed her concerns to him and asked for advice, and Merton gave it. Under an avalanche of correspondence, Merton not only took the time to respond to a teenager but also seemed to relish doing so, engaging her as a person who had something worthwhile to say and who could be a friend.

This pattern is repeated frequently in his correspondence with young people. To Susan Neer, a high school student in Missouri, Merton writes honestly and eloquently about racism (*RJ*, 329–30); to Jim Frost, a high school student in Iowa, Merton writes about what the environment means to him (*RJ*, 330); to Tony Boyd, a seventh-grader in Kentucky, Merton writes playfully about music, for example, "I like Johnny Cash" (*RJ*, 346); and to Roberto Gri, a young Italian student, Merton gives advice about how to study (*RJ*, 334). One of his more remarkable letters is the one he wrote to Susan Chapulis, a sixth-grader in Connecticut, to whom Merton gives a description of the monastic life and also guidance on how to cultivate a life of prayer. "I suggest that you sometimes be quiet and think how good a thing it is that you are loved by God who is infinite and who wants you to be supremely happy and who in fact is going to make you supremely happy" (*RJ*, 351). "Never write down to anyone," Merton says in a letter to a young, aspiring writer from Ireland, and his letters to young people indicate how well he took his own advice (*RJ*, 336).

HUMILITY IN DIRECTION

Merton frequently received letters asking for guidance and direction, and he endeavored to answer as many as he could. One of those to whom Merton gave frequent guidance was Jim Forest, the peace activist to whom I referred at the beginning of this essay. The 1960s were, of course, a tumultuous time for the peace movement in the United States. Forest, at the time a young Catholic who began his work with Dorothy Day at the Catholic Worker and later founded the Catholic Peace Fellowship, found in Merton someone who took an extraordinary interest in what he was doing.

In his book *The Root of War Is Fear*, Forest describes a letter he received from Merton during a particularly dark period of his life. Early in 1966, Forest was dealing with the disintegration of his marriage, the self-immolation of a young activist—Roger LaPorte—that shocked the peace movement, and growing discouragement about his own work. In February, Forest wrote to Merton that he was "in a rather bleak mood," and in an anguished tone, he shared with Merton that he was exhausted and despairing and felt "like an ant climbing a cliff" in his work for peace.[4] He ends the letter asking for guidance.

Merton's reply is one of the longest letters in his correspondence. It contains no platitudes, no attempt to soothe with empty words of reassurance. Merton takes Forest's despair seriously, but doesn't pretend that he has answers: "I don't have magic solutions for bleak moods: if I did I would use them on my own which are habitually pretty bleak too" (*HGL*, 294). Instead, Merton becomes present to Forest, taking his despair upon himself and walking him through it by offering another lens into his situation, the lens of a contemplative whose life revolved around the steady witness of solitude and silence in a world of action and chaos. Knowing that the temptation of the activist is to settle for nothing less than the immediate transformation of the world and that despair is the inevitable consequence when such transformation fails to occur, Merton encouraged Forest to adopt a different approach:

> [D]o not depend on the hope of results. When you are doing the sort of work you have taken on, essentially an apostolic work, you may have to face the fact that your work will be apparently worthless and even achieve no result at all, if not perhaps results opposite to what you expect. As you get used to this idea you start more and more to concentrate not on the results but on the value, the rightness, the truth of the work itself. . . . In the end, as you yourself mention in passing, it is the reality of personal relationships that saves everything. (*HGL*, 294)

Merton was accustomed to people challenging him to leave the monastery to do something active to change the world, and while he understood this impulse, he also understood that the contemplative life quietly and methodically works to change the world by witnessing to another way of being. The life itself was its own justification. Merton uses this logic to help Forest understand the value of his work, even in the midst of his despair. Merton endeavors to redirect Forest's focus away from immediate results and toward the beauty and worth of his "apostolic work" and to recognize that at the heart of this work must be the fostering of genuine relationships. Forest, like Merton, was offering to the world another way of being, the way of love. Therefore, Merton writes, "All the good you will do will come not from you but from the fact that you have allowed yourself, in the obedience of faith, to be used by God's love" (*HGL*, 296).

Forest describes Merton's letter as "the most helpful letter I've ever received." "From time to time," Forest writes, "when the sky was turning starless black, I reread it."[5] It became so valuable to him that he shared it with his colleagues and other close friends when they too felt burned out from their seemingly fruitless work. Isolated from the world in the woods of Kentucky, Merton entered fully into his friend's despair, listening to him carefully and standing alongside him to gaze this despair squarely in the face. By doing so, by sharing in and so validating Forest's emotions, Merton was able to give his friend a different perspective on his work, emphasizing the divine value of that work regardless of the outcome. It is no wonder that Forest often found himself and his work so validated by Merton that he carried the most recent letter he received from him in his shirt pocket.[6]

CONCLUSION: "WE ARE BOTH CHRIST"

In 1958, a schoolteacher in England named John Harris began a correspondence with Merton. Harris initially wrote to Merton at the behest of Boris Pasternak, to whom Harris had written after reading *Doctor Zhivago*. Harris soon found in Merton someone to whom he could turn with theological questions and personal dilemmas. Merton evidently sensed in Harris a reticence to bother the monk with his issues, so Merton concludes his second letter to Harris as follows:

> Do not hesitate to write if there is anything I can do for you. . . . The important thing is who are you: you are not a "man with a problem," or a person trying to figure something out, you are Harris, in Devonshire . . . you are you and that is the important thing. . . . [W]hen "I"

enter into a dialogue with "you" and each of us knows
who is speaking, it turns out that we are both Christ.
This, being seen in a very simple and "natural" light,
is the beginning and almost the fullness of everything.
Everything is in it somewhere. (*HGL*, 387)

These words encapsulate Merton's understanding of friendship and
maintaining friendship through correspondence. He endeavored
to see his correspondents, not as people with this issue or that concern, but as *people*. He sought to engage his friends as they were,
to meet them on their own terms. Over and over in his writings,
Merton emphasizes the importance of viewing all people through
the lens of the Incarnation, by which he means not only that we
must see how profoundly all are loved by God, but also that we
need to see Christ in each and every person. It is this insight that
lay at the heart of Merton's famous Fourth and Walnut experience, when he "suddenly saw the secret beauty" of those around
him on that street corner in Louisville (*CGB*, 154). And it is this
insight that is instantiated in his correspondence. Merton was able
to begin and maintain friendships through his correspondence
because he had the humility to see Christ in those to whom he
wrote, and to love them accordingly. In turn, his correspondents
came to see Christ in Merton.

5.

Our Expanded Religious and Spiritual Horizons

Kevin Hunt, O.C.S.O. Sensei

The church that Thomas Merton joined in the late 1930s was a church that was extremely parochial. For most Catholics, a very large part of their lives was centered on their local parish; it was the focus not only of their religious practice but also of much of their social life. The majority of Catholics were first- or second-generation Americans, they were the children or grandchildren of immigrants. Many of the Catholic churches were ethnic. It was not unusual to find a French Canadian church built within a couple of city blocks of the Irish Catholic church. In a small town, there might be a church for Polish Catholics, German Catholics, or Portuguese Catholics. Each of these churches most likely had its own school and social center. All of them used the same Latin liturgy but taught and preached in the language of their predominant ethnic group. It was not unusual for Catholics of one ethnic group to have little social interaction with Catholics of another.

With the Second World War, this began to change. Men especially were taken out of their ethnic social situations and had to live and mingle with other American men whom they would not have ordinarily encountered. The war sent thousands of young men to parts of the world that they had barely heard of, and surely had not visited—traveling to places like India and China and, when the war was over, stationed as occupation forces in Japan and Korea. This exposed them to cultures and religions that they might have only seen before in a *National Geographic* magazine. Many of these men returned to the United States with insights into the religious values of such cultures.

Once the war ended, the G.I. Bill presented more opportunities to the men who had served. Veterans who might not have been able to go to college were offered higher education. For many, this opened up possibilities that they would not have otherwise considered. It was precisely this generation and its younger siblings that Thomas Merton influenced first with his writings.

The general thrust in books on asceticism and mysticism in those days—before World War II—was that mystical graces and advanced states of prayer were rarely to be found, even among Catholics who were priests and religious. The usual direction given to anyone interested in prayer was simply to follow the ordinary practices of the Catholic Church, such as the Rosary, the Stations of the Cross, and novenas. Any departure from such common devotions was very risky and was discouraged. The most common form of meditation taught to seminarians and young religious was a rigid sort of rational reflection on the life of Jesus and the saints.

It was also genuinely accepted in Catholic teaching on prayer and spirituality of that time that true prayer and mystical experience were only found in the Catholic Church. The so-called "mystical experiences" found in other religious traditions were either illusions or deceptions of the evil spirits.

European and American Christians had little or no knowledge or understanding, on the whole, of the meditative traditions of India or East Asia. The first Parliament of the World's Religions, held in Chicago in 1893 as part of the World Columbian Exposition, was the first time that Americans had the opportunity to learn such traditions. But, despite the presence of a Catholic bishop (P. A. Feehan), who was on the preparatory board for the parliament, and James Cardinal Gibbons, who gave the opening invocation, American Christians, especially Catholics, mostly ignored what happened in Chicago.

The Indian and East Asian meditation teachers there, however, were of the highest caliber. Swami Vivekananda represented the Vedanta Hindu tradition. Buddhist teachers included Dharmapala (Theravada) and Soyen Shaku (Zen tradition), whose translator, D. T. Suzuki, later corresponded with Thomas Merton. Virchand Gandhi represented the Jains, and Mohammed A. R. Webb, an English convert, represented Islam. This was the first opportunity for American Christians to encounter non-Christian religions, as well as to encounter great teachers of meditation. All of the conservative and most of the mainline Protestant churches and their leaders rejected the whole idea of the World's Parliament of Religions, as did the Archbishop of Canterbury and most of the Catholic hierarchy. The well-known English Catholic author G. K. Chesterton wrote in his book *The Everlasting Man* that the parliament was "a pantheon for pantheists."

In general, there was not much real knowledge of Asian traditions of meditation back then. But after World War II, many of those military men that had had the opportunity to see such practices firsthand began to spread their knowledge in America and Europe. Some of the Asian teachers of meditation not only began to teach Europeans but also traveled to Europe and America. Perhaps the best known of these teachers was Maharishi Mahesh Yogi, who developed what came to be known as Transcendental Meditation. Both his fame and Transcendental Meditation were greatly enhanced by the Maharishi's relationship with the Beatles. (He was briefly their "spiritual advisor" in 1967.)

In the late 1960s and early 1970s, some of the students of Transcendental Meditation went to St. Joseph's Abbey in Spencer, Massachusetts, and introduced TM to the monks. The practice of TM alongside the deep reading of the Desert Fathers led Fathers William Meninger, Basil Pennington, and Thomas Keating to formulate the practice of centering prayer. Centering prayer has become one of the major focuses in the revitalization of meditation in the Church today.

Similarly, English Benedictine John Main experienced the Hindu traditions of meditation while he worked in the British Colonial Office in Malaya. There he met Swami Satyananda, who taught him to meditate using a Christian mantra. Later, he utilized that experience to develop a Christian form of meditation using Christian mantras, and taught that method to many in England, continental Europe, and Canada. He started the World Community for Christian Meditation, which remains very active in interreligious dialogue.

But Catholics were generally satisfied with who they were, seeing little need to expand their horizons in the ways that people like Fathers Meninger, Pennington, and Keating did. Although large segments of Eastern European Catholicism had been lost behind the iron curtain, in the United States there was a sense of security and satisfaction. We could see how the Catholic Church had come of age in our society. Our parishes were vibrant; rare was the church that did not have a number of masses every Sunday, and attendance was high. Churches had schools that rivaled those of the public systems. Our seminaries and houses of religious formation filled to overflowing. One of the most popular television personalities was Bishop Fulton Sheen, who gave talks on the teachings of the Church.

Then Thomas Merton's *The Seven Storey Mountain* quickly became a best seller. Reviewers compared it to John Henry Newman's *Apologia Pro Vita Sua*. Merton's autobiography spoke to those men and women of the post–World War II era. Although Merton had never been in the military, nor experienced the horrors of war firsthand, his disillusionment with twentieth-century society and its largely bankrupt ideals spoke to those who had suffered in the war.

The Seven Storey Mountain was published in 1948 and was followed the next year by *Seeds of Contemplation*. In the author's note at the beginning of that book, Merton hit a note that resonated in many hearts: "Yet since the interior life and contemplation are things we need most of all—I speak only of the kind of contemplation that springs from the love of God—the kind of considerations written in these pages ought to be something for which everybody, and not only monks, would have a great hunger in our time" (*NSC*, xix). A great hunger was there, and now it was out in the open. Merton realized that such a hunger was found not just in those who felt a call to go into the monastery, but in everyone. And in that slim book, Merton shared reflections on prayer and its difficulties that anyone, inside the monastery or outside, can experience. Early in *Seeds of Contemplation*, which was later revised by Merton and retitled *New Seeds of Contemplation*, he opens the experience of contemplation to everyone: "Every moment and every event of every man's life on earth plants something in his soul. For just as the wind carries thousands of invisible and visible winged seeds, so the stream of time brings with it germs of spiritual vitality that come to rest imperceptibly in the minds and wills of men. Most of these unnumbered seeds perish and are lost because men are unprepared to receive them" (*NSC*, 14).

Underlying the euphoria following the winning of World War II was a discontent with the norms and values articulated by the so-called American dream. This discontent had many people searching for reasons for existence beyond a two-car garage and a good chicken dinner on Sunday. In Europe, the postwar malaise expressed itself in a negative existentialism along with a sense that the old regime had failed. Perhaps Marxism was the solution. But then the Soviet Union's suppression of the Hungarian Revolution of 1956 demonstrated to the world that the Soviet form of Marxism was just another form of imperialism.

Merton's writings found a fertile field in both America and Europe. The contemplative life, whether lived in a monastery or in the world, was suddenly opened to everyone. Merton had a curiosity about this life of prayer and meditation that was stoked by his work with the novices and juniors of his own monastery. This curiosity of Merton and others like him diminished the traditional fears created by the years of the Counter-Reformation and the challenges of modern nationalism and the sciences. It was especially Merton's essays and correspondence with teachers of meditation from other religious traditions that nurtured a sense of confidence even among Catholic traditionalists, which then opened them to study and even practice other forms of meditation.

—— —— —— —— —— —— —— —— —— —— ——

I entered St. Joseph's Abbey in Spencer, Massachusetts, in 1953. Although I had developed an interest in Catholic monasticism and meditation before reading Merton, his books and essays were a source of encouragement and intellectual curiosity.

Upon entering the monastery, I found that there was a sense of openness to investigate and even practice the ways of meditation that interested you. I was taught that liberty of spirit was encouraged and supported. For example, I can remember going to my novice director and telling him of my difficulties with the more traditional practices of meditation. He encouraged me to seek a simpler form of prayer. My curiosity then led me to the earliest practices witnessed in such books as the writings of the first Christian monks in the Egyptian desert and the Fertile Crescent. A little book entitled *The Way of a Pilgrim* also instructed me in the practice of the continual recitation of the name of Jesus. This practice has continued to be part of my life some sixty years later.

When I first entered the monastery, the tradition was that the monastic could not sit in church for meditation. One either knelt or stood. The most common medical complaint among the younger monks was "housemaid's knee." It was only in the 1950s that we were permitted to use a chair for prayer and meditation. The result, at least in my experience, was that the majority of the young monastics promptly fell asleep.

In the early 1960s, I was sent to help in the construction of a new monastery in Argentina. At that time, I had a growing curiosity about the forms of meditation that were practiced in the non-Christian meditative traditions of India and East Asia. It was during my first year in Argentina that a visitor to the monastery gave me a Spanish translation of a book originally written in German and translated into English with the title *The Art of the Archer*. It was the first book that I read about how to practice Zen meditation. The author describes how Zen meditation was foundational to the practice of archery in Japan. I was intrigued by the description of the way Zen Buddhist monastics in Japan perform their meditation. I thought that if I were to sit in that cross-legged position, it would be so uncomfortable that I would not be able to fall asleep. I was also intrigued by the koan, a Zen question that the author presented as an example of what Zen monks focus on during their meditation. From my reading of Thomas Merton and

D. T. Suzuki, I knew somewhat what a koan was, but this was the first time that I had encountered a practical explanation of using a koan in meditation. That particular koan was the famous, "What face did you have before you were conceived?"

So I gathered and folded up several blankets to sit on during my meditation. Some of the other monks were a bit disconcerted by my sitting in that way, so the superior gave me permission to do my meditation in a small side chapel. For the next five or six years I sat on my blankets, focused on my breath, and once in a while repeated that koan to myself. I remember some of the other monks being upset by what I was doing. There were remarks such as, "Are you trying to be a Buddhist monk or a Christian monk?" But on the whole, my brothers were content to let me do my thing.

During those years that I sat on my blankets and watched my breath and repeated the koan, nothing happened. All I got out of the practice were painful legs and an aching back. One day I decided to give up on this practice and rejoin my brothers in the main church and just repeat the Jesus prayer. So I uncurled my legs and stood up. But at that moment, in the motion of standing, I suddenly realized the face that I had before I was conceived. I was completely bewildered by what happened. I had no one that I could talk to about this experience, so I just continued my practice.

A couple of years later, I returned to St. Joseph's Abbey. My superior gave me permission to visit a Zen master in the New York area, but I was unsuccessful in obtaining an interview. I just continued my practice.

After another couple of years, I was traveling with another monk through Princeton, New Jersey, when my companion asked if we could stop for a moment and see his friend, a nun who ran a boarding school nearby. I agreed, and we drove to the school. As we were chatting, the sister mentioned that a Zen group had rented the school for a week of retreat. When I showed interest, the nun offered to introduce the teacher. Shortly thereafter, a small Japanese man dressed in the traditional robes of a Zen teacher (*rōshi*) came out with his assistant, who was interpreting for him. When we identified ourselves as Catholic monastics, the *rōshi*, Joshu Sasaki Roshi, said that he knew that there were Christian monastics but thought that they were only to be found in Europe. We invited him to visit our monastery, and he quickly accepted.

Several weeks later, the Roshi came to Spencer and spoke to the community about Zen practice. His talk led to an invitation to return and lead a Zen retreat for two days. A large number of monks participated and showed interest in continuing the experience. (The community had already experienced TM.) Ultimately, the Roshi returned regularly for about ten years to continue leading us in Zen practice. In addition, I went to the Roshi's meditation center at Mt. Baldy near Los Angeles for three intense training periods (ninety days) during that time. Later on, I also participated in several training periods at the Providence Zen Center in Cumberland, Rhode Island, of the Korean Zen Buddhist tradition.

The Spencer monastery had developed over the years a relationship with the Barre Center for Buddhist Studies. Some of our monks participated in interreligious programs at the center. On one occasion, several of us were invited to attend a conference on the meaning of the Passion presented by Robert Kennedy, S.J., a recognized Zen teacher. As I was chatting with Father Kennedy after the presentation, he mentioned that he would soon be giving a Zen retreat at St. Benedict's Monastery in Snowmass, Colorado. I and another monk of Spencer received permission to attend that retreat. Toward the end of the retreat (*sesshin*), I asked Father Kennedy if he would take me as one of his students. He agreed. I then worked with Father Kennedy for a number of years. I finally asked for a leave of absence from the monastery to live at his *zendō* in Jersey City so as to have a more intense practice with him. I was given permission to do so for a year and a half, and at the end of that time Father Kennedy made me a Zen teacher.

I doubt that any of my meditation journeys would have been possible without the writings and life of Thomas Merton. Merton's obedience to his superiors (an obedience that he found very difficult at times) demonstrated in a real way his overcoming of his "false self" and the truth of his contemplative experience. That experience was a journey into mystery. Perhaps it was this lived witness of the contemplative life as a journey into mystery that makes Merton such a model for people today.

Meditation is part and parcel of modern-day experience. It can be found in a multitude of disciplines and in almost any situation. It is the subject of scientific experimentation and market research. Some business firms have their associates participate in retreats during which meditation is taught and encouraged. In medicine, meditation is prescribed to lower the possibility of heart attack; in psychiatry, it has been found to reduce stress. It can be found as part of a child's school day. It is taught in prisons, where it reduces incidents of violence. Transcendental Meditation or zazen and other forms of meditation are part of chaplaincy programs in hospitals and schools.

Meditation is not necessarily associated with any particular religion. Many meditators will tell you that they are not religious, but are spiritual. It is common to find participants in meditation groups that come from different religious traditions. Jews sit alongside Christians, Muslims alongside atheists and agnostics.

It really doesn't matter why one begins to meditate. I know people who meditate to reduce stress or to relax after work. Some start because of simple curiosity. One man I know had experimented with LSD in college. His experience made him realize that there was more to reality than science could explain. He didn't particularly like the side effects of LSD, so he decided to see if meditation might not work. He is still at it after forty years. A woman I know started to meditate because her boyfriend experimented with it. The boyfriend gave up, but she continued to meditate and gave up the boyfriend.

There are many forms of meditation: the repetition of a mantra, watching the breath, reasoning, and use of the imagination. Some are very physical: making prostrations, walking, or sitting still. About the only constant (as a wise old monk said many years ago) is that real meditation will tend to become quieter and simpler.

As mentioned above, the Hindu practice of the mantra has already become part of the practice of the Church. Buddhist methods of meditation are also being utilized by Christians interested in meditation and contemplation. There are Christian forms of insight meditation, notably those developed by Mary Jo Meadow and Father Kevin Culigan. Zen, of course, has a number of Christian teachers who have experience from many different Zen schools and traditions.

It would be a mistake to think that these different methods of meditation that come from Asian meditative traditions are simply given the name Christian but remain substantially Hindu or Buddhist. Rather, they represent a true marriage of Christian tradition and a practice from another tradition. This happened at least twice before in the history of Christianity. The first time was the acceptance of Greek philosophy in the early Church through the efforts of men such as Justin Martyr, Origen, and the Cappadocians. The second was the "baptizing" of Aristotle during the Middle Ages by the efforts of Albert the Great and Thomas Aquinas. Recall that many great Christian philosophers rejected Aristotle because they thought that he did not believe in God. Many Christians today react the same way to the Buddha.

Actually, the current effort to Christianize meditative practices that developed in other religious traditions goes far beyond dressing those practices in a white baptismal robe. Father Kevin

Culligan and Mary Jo Meadow, for instance, both see insight meditation as a way of penetrating more deeply and understanding more clearly what Carmelite spirituality teaches, especially through John of the Cross. Personally, I recall a number of conversations with Father William Meninger on using TM as a vehicle to experiencing the meditation insights of *The Cloud of Unknowing*. And, of course, I would talk with Thomas Keating (he was my abbot at the time) about it when I saw him.

In the 1950s and 1960s, the travel books by H. V. Morton were popular in contemplative monasteries, especially his journeys in the Middle East. The ordinary monk of the time didn't have much of an opportunity to visit exotic and interesting places like the Holy Land or Egypt, so books like *In the Steps of St. Paul* at least gave us some idea of where Jesus lived. In one of his books, Morton tells of visiting the Coptic monasteries of Egypt. His stories of how these monks lived enthralled me. He recounts that these monks would sit on low benches made of reeds to pray. When they got tired, they had low staffs in the shape of a T that they would lean on. I wondered if they had the same problem with sleep, which was the bane of my attempts to meditate, but I could not figure out a way to make such a bench or staff. When I read how the Buddhist monks sat in meditation, I knew I had found a possible solution.

One of the difficulties that people experience today is a certain mental fatigue arising from the attention that many jobs demand. Our minds are in an active mode nearly all day. We are subjected to a ceaseless bombardment of information, of sense input, and decision making. Our society is filled with dangers and violence. At the time of meditation, we carry all this baggage into our sacred space. People are looking for stillness and peace. Our Western prayer practices do not easily provide quiet moments and space for the heart to be at peace. Many Asian meditation practices are helpful to find and utilize a peaceful mind and heart.

There is also the reality that the consumer orientation of the West ultimately proves to be unsatisfactory. No matter how successful our career might be, no matter how much money we have in the bank, our hearts are not at peace. St. Augustine's dictum, "Our hearts are restless until they rest in Thee," is experienced day in and day out.

In his book *The Varieties of Religious Experience*, William James says that the simplest definition of mysticism is "awareness of the presence of God." I would add that awareness of nonpresence of God, or emptiness, or mystery, is also mysticism. Everyone is a mystic or contemplative; it's just that the majority of us are unaware of it.

The different methods of prayer and meditation offer a way for each of us to enter into and realize who and what we really are. One of the most valuable teachings on meditation I ever heard was "Try, just try."

6.

What It Means to Be a Person of Dialogue

Daniel P. Horan, O.F.M.

When Pope Francis addressed a historic joint session of the United States Congress during his Apostolic Visit on September 24, 2015, he drew on the wisdom and example of four individuals to frame his remarks to the American people. Noting that the year 2015 marked significant anniversaries of "several great Americans," the Bishop of Rome explained "These men and women offer us a way of seeing and interpreting reality. In honoring their memory, we are inspired, even amid conflicts, and in the here and now of each day, to draw upon our deepest cultural reserves."[1] He selected four key figures: Abraham Lincoln, Martin Luther King Jr., Dorothy Day, and Thomas Merton

Pope Francis explained his selection of the Trappist monk and Catholic priest, who was both a spiritual writer and social critic, by stating: "Merton was above all a man of prayer, a thinker who challenged the certitudes of his time and opened new horizons for souls and for the Church. He was also a man of dialogue, a promoter of peace between peoples and religions." He added that Merton was an exemplar of "the capacity for dialogue and openness to God."

Pope Francis's enthusiastic recommendation of Merton leads us to consider several implications that his brief address to Congress leaves unaddressed. What exactly does it mean to be a person of dialogue? How does one go about engaging in authentic dialogue? In what contexts does or should dialogue take place? And how may Merton provide us with insights into becoming women and men of dialogue who, like him, serve the world and Church as promoters of peace between peoples and religions?

At a time in which the individual is celebrated at the expense of the community, social media connects people superficially but creates a relational gap, and personal views related to politics, ethics, and religion have grown exceptionally polarized, the call Pope Francis continually makes for collaboration, community, and civility is especially timely. For Merton, this division and increasing isolation, even in his time fifty years ago, was a pressing concern. On numerous occasions he wrote about the necessity to seek a way of living other than as a "society of isolated individuals"—that we are called to engage with one another on a profound level in order to build communities of persons and not merely collections of individuals. Concerning the world of isolated individuals, Merton explains that "they do not know that reality is to be sought not in division but in unity, for we are 'members of one another' . . . the one who lives in division is not a person but only an 'individual'" (*NSC*, 47–48).

Pursuing answers to all of these questions, I want to explore four areas in which Merton engaged in dialogue and invites us to do likewise: dialogue with God, dialogue with culture, dialogue with society, and dialogue with religions. Though this is hardly an exhaustive treatment of the manifold ways Merton's life, writings, and legacy provide us with insight about developing relationships rooted in justice, peace, and mutuality, it is my hope that it offers a contribution to the discussion that Pope Francis invited us to consider during his first visit to the United States.

DIALOGUE WITH GOD

If people know of Thomas Merton, it's likely they know about his writings on the spiritual life, prayer, or contemplation. In the early decades of Merton's religious life, the 1940s and 1950s, his contribution to Catholic spirituality was distinctive in that he extended an invitation to all women and men to develop a life of prayer and faith. Today such an observation might appear obvious, but prior to the Second Vatican Council (1962–1965), Roman Catholics generally understood the life of prayer and contemplation to belong to the "professional religious"—nuns, priests, monks, and so forth—and not to the laity. Merton upended that presumption, suggesting that the world in which we find ourselves is in fact a world in which God seeks connection and relationship with all people. Merton suggested that "[t]he ever-changing reality in the midst of which we live should awaken us to the possibility of an uninterrupted dialogue with God" (*NSC*, 14). In contrast to the belief that prayer is something that operates according to our terms or requires of us a commitment to consecrated religious life, Merton invited all people to consider that God *seeks us first* and that we can cultivate practices of attunement to that loving presence of God already always near us. "We must learn," Merton wrote, "to realize that the love of God seeks us in every situation, and seeks our good. His inscrutable love seeks our awakening" (*NSC*, 15). If we imagine prayer as a two-way street, then we can rest assured that God is doing God's part in that form of relational communication. It is you and I that remain the inactive partners in our respective dialogues with God, and Merton challenges us to do our part to carry on the conversation with our Creator.

As if to echo the psalmist who proclaims "God is in the city" in Psalm 46, Merton asserts that God's presence is not limited to the traditionally "churchy" locations we typically imagine. Instead, Merton's spiritual vision is shaped by the longstanding Christian tradition that unabashedly announces God's presence everywhere in creation: "It is God's love that speaks to me in the birds and streams; but also behind the clamor of the city God speaks to me in His judgments, and all these things are seeds sent to me from His will" (*NSC*, 17). The dialogue, the conversation, and the *prayer* can take place anywhere and everywhere, and not just on Sunday mornings at Mass in the parish.

For Merton, the intimacy of the dialogue with God is beyond all other forms of closeness and relationship. The influence of St. Augustine's spiritual reflections on Merton's writing is evident in this way. Augustine famously wrote in Book III of his spiritual autobiography, *Confessions*, "God is the one closer to us than we are to ourselves."[2] Merton expands on this intuition when discussing the nature of the dialogue with God in contemplation.

> Contemplation is also the response to a call: a call from Him Who has no voice, and yet Who speaks everything that is, and Who, most of all, speaks in the depths of our own being: for we ourselves are words of His. But we are words that are meant to respond to him, to answer to Him, to echo Him, and even in some way to contain Him and signify Him. Contemplation is this echo. It is a deep resonance in the inmost center of our spirit in which our very life loses its separate voice and re-sounds with the majesty and the mercy of the Hidden and Loving One. (*NSC*, 3)

So close is God's presence to us that it is like an unspoken, unmediated, and uncomplicated conversation or dialogue.

The difficulty of this dialogue with God is what Merton calls the contemplative awakening; that is, we must be open and attuned to the invitation of relationship that God extends to us at all times. When we awaken to the mystery of God's presence in our lives, this is at once the beginning of dialogue with God and the inauguration of our discovery of our *true self.* For Merton, dialogue with God is both a discovery of who God really is and the discovery of who we really are: "The secret of my identity is hidden in the love and mercy of God" (*NSC,* 35). Though modern societies and popular cultures tell us that we need to construct our identities and shape our personal futures, Merton insists that who we really are is known to God alone, for God loved each of us into existence individually and in our particularity. We cannot merely happen upon or discover our true selves by ourselves. "For although I can know something of God's existence and nature by my own reason, there is no human and rational way in which I can arrive at this contact, that possession of Him, which will be the discovery of Who He really is and Who I am in Him" (*NSC,* 36).

Merton's encouraging challenge for all of us is to embrace a life of prayer and contemplation as an invitation to cultivate dialogue with God. This allows us to come to know the Creator better and, ultimately, to discover our true identity. In a preface he wrote to a collection of prayers in 1961, Merton summarizes what a dialogue with God looks like and leads to: "Prayer is not only the 'lifting up of the mind and heart to God,' but it is also the response to God within us, the discovery of God within us; it leads ultimately to the discovery and fulfilment of our own true being in God."[3] This effort is not only for a few and the religious elite but also for every member of the human family.

DIALOGUE WITH CULTURE

On the relationship between an individual and culture, theologian Orlando Espín once wrote, "We are in culture as in a womb from which there is no birth, because we are already born into it."[4] Although difficult to articulate, culture is an inescapable reality and condition of human existence. We are born into it, it shapes our imaginations and dreams, and informs our fears and prejudices. In our modern sense, culture has several components, including a universal dimension (nobody exists outside one or more cultures), variation among social groups (culture can be seen as an attribute of each particular group), and an entire way of life (it is made of social habits and institutions, rituals, beliefs, values, and so on).[5] For our purposes, let's consider culture as that "womb," or context in which Merton found himself and which helped shape his particular horizon.

In addition to a dialogue with God marked by contemplative prayer, Merton also engaged in and encouraged others to engage in a dialogue with culture—both their own and that of others. Patrick O'Connell explains, "Thomas Merton was both committed to the values of his own culture and open to the contributions of other cultures and an advocate of what he called 'transcultural consciousness.'"[6] This term "transcultural consciousness" summarizes Merton's commitment to the dialogue between his own culture and familiar traditions and those cultures and traditions of other women and men from around the globe. He firmly believed that one could not dialogue with another culture or tradition without first being deeply grounded in one's own. Without an adequate rooting in a particular intellectual and artistic heritage, any attempt to engage another would be not a dialogue but a unidirectional monologue—it could lead to the pilfering of another culture without anything to provide in return. To avoid this intercultural pitfall, Merton believed that, in the words of O'Connell, one had to "become conversant with one's own culture . . . [that is,] to recognize its shortcomings and distortions, its past sins, its current problems, its future threats." Merton believed that viewing one's own context with a critical lens was a form of respect, love, and fidelity for that which was inherited from previous generations and communities.

In *Conjectures of a Guilty Bystander*, Merton offers a number of reflections on both his own cultural background—that of a European-born white man who emigrated to the United States and is now a member of a Roman Catholic religious community—and his forays into learning more about other cultures. Regarding his own culture, Merton recognized both the strengths and weaknesses that arise within the Euro-American context: "Our ability to see ourselves objectively and to criticize our own actions, our own failings, is the source of a very real strength. But to those who fear truth, who have begun to forget the genuine Western heritage and to become immersed in crude materialism without spirit, this critical tendency presents the greatest danger" (*CGB*, 69). He goes on to caution against what he perceives to be a cultural trend toward overreliance on technology and consumerism, which weakens the uniqueness and authenticity of cultural particularity. He insists that one must critically engage with one's heritage so as to appreciate what has been handed on from previous generations as well as identify that which is emerging in the present.

Visual and performing arts, literature and poetry, religion and mythology, history and narrative, language and expression all come together to form what Merton recognized as the matrix of a culture. Having sought to secure his own appreciation for and understanding of his cultural foundation as best as he could, he then turned toward others with a spirit of openness. He approached these dialogues in a particular way. O'Connell notes, "It is particularly important, in Merton's view, to comprehend other civilizations on their own terms, not to make any premature attempt at assimilation, to reject the temptation to incorporate congenial elements

of another culture into one's own worldview and discard the rest."
Merton's concern was to avoid syncretism, the piecemeal selection
of what strikes one as subjectively appealing while overlooking or
rejecting those aspects of a tradition that seem unattractive, or what
is often referred to today as "cultural appropriation" (the uncriti-
cal mimicry or adaptation of cultural characteristics or behaviors
without sufficient context or understanding).

A touchstone of authentic dialogue between cultures is the
profound appreciation for the integrity of the particular culture
or tradition. The goal is "to appreciate the core values of another
tradition . . . the sympathetic effort to perceive the world from
the standpoint of another, to enter as far as possible into that
framework." Merton always understood this dialogue in a spiritual
dimension, recognizing, "On its deepest level, this receptivity is
an openness to the divine present within the other." In this way,
Merton at first anticipated and then reflected the wisdom of the
Second Vatican Council in which the Roman Catholic Church
proclaimed that the Church rejects nothing that is true or good
in other religions or cultures.[7]

This sort of dialogue presumes a real relationship characterized
by vulnerability and humility. The vulnerability emerges in the risk
of being misunderstood, while the humility rests in the conviction
that one's culture does not have a monopoly on what is good or
true. Dialogue with culture also presupposes the patience necessary
to listen, discern, and discuss within a community of difference.
One must resist the fear of what is different or perceived as foreign; or, more bluntly, one must resist the temptation to espouse
xenophobic attitudes and assumptions. The result is the possibility
of mutual enrichment and a return to one's own cultural context
with greater appreciation.

In *Mystics and Zen Masters*, Merton draws on the possibility of
Western European and North American engagement with Eastern
cultures and traditions to highlight exactly this point about mutual

enrichment. "The cultural heritage of Asia has as much right to be studied in our colleges as the cultural heritage of Greece and Rome," he writes, adding, "If the West can recognize that contact with Eastern thought can renew our appreciation for our own cultural heritage, a product of the fusion of the Judeo-Christian religion with Greco-Roman culture, then it will be easier to defend that heritage, not only in Asia but in the West as well" (*MZM*, 45–46).

Merton's understanding of what it means to become a better Christian is tied to this understanding of what it means to become a better human person generally. He advises that we ground ourselves in the depths of our cultural contexts and also express openness to other cultures and traditions.

DIALOGUE WITH SOCIETY

In his encomium for Merton before the joint session of Congress, Pope Francis emphasized that Merton was "a thinker who challenged the certitudes of his time and opened new horizons for souls and for the Church."[8] One of the ways Merton "challenged the certitudes of his time" was by being a public intellectual and a social critic. Unlike many newspaper columnists or university professors, Merton's public intellectualism didn't originate in the traditional venues or typically appear in the usual style of notable commentators. He was a monk and priest whose commitment to a religious life of prayer and work (*ora et labora*) remained rooted in a particular and circumscribed geographic place. For this reason, he might not have been the most traveled observer of social mores and his contemporary zeitgeist. He nevertheless had a sense of the collective cultural pulse and recognized the everyday realities of his contemporaries. His commitment to seeing the "signs of the times" and then interpreting them "in light of the Gospel" (*Gaudium et Spes* 4) governed his dialogue with society, offering a view from the margins that was unique. Merton's distinctive location made him

a kind of resident alien in the American context, attuned to the
ethos of his age, which—particularly in the 1950s and 1960s—was
consumed with matters of violence and racism.[9]

Whereas culture is an internalized reality, a "womb" that always
already surrounds us and from which we cannot escape, society
can be understood as the normative structuring of communities
outside of us. Cultures remain understandably intangible and
difficult to identify clearly. Societies, on the other hand, are established and systemically organized. Merton's dialogue with society
began by grounding himself in his own tradition and social location. He anticipated what Vatican II would teach regarding how
to interpret the current events and environment once recognized
according to the "light of the Gospel." As a result, his writings on
war and racism were prescient, while remaining prophetic and
deeply Christian.

He wrote at great length about the Vietnam conflict, nuclear
weapons, and other corporate and individual acts of violence. In
the posthumously published *Contemplation in a World of Action*,
Merton reflected on the way that his birth at a particular point in
history shaped his experience and outlook:

> That I should be born in 1915, that I should be the
> contemporary of Auschwitz, Hiroshima, Vietnam, and
> the Watts riots, are things about which I was not first
> consulted. Yet they are also events in which, whether
> I like it or not, I am deeply and personally involved.
> The "world" is not just a physical space traversed by jet
> planes and full of people running in all directions. It
> is a complex of responsibilities and options made out
> of the loves, the hates, the fears, the joys, the hopes,
> the greed, the cruelty, the kindness, the faith, the trust,
> the suspicion of all. In the last analysis, if there is war
> because nobody trusts anybody, this is in part because I
> myself am defensive, suspicious, untrusting, and intent

> on making other people conform themselves to my
> particular brand of death wish. (*CWA*, 143)

In this way he lays out his motivation for engagement with broader society. In stark contrast to the common-sense logic of religious life at the time, governed by a *fuga mundi* ("fleeing the world") mentality, Merton deliberately occupied a place at the margins as someone who remained in touch with and connected to the world—if not exactly "of the world," to use an oft-quoted religious phrase.

Rooted in his conviction that authentic gospel life demanded a radical nonviolent attitude toward conflict, Merton's dialogue with social actors and about the circumstances of his time often took on a critical hue. As James Baker explains, "When Thomas Merton emerged from his monastic hideaway in the early 1950s and looked again upon the America which he had adopted, he saw a land filled with violence, a society whose personality and nature were molded by its violent past and whose ability to change its violent present might cause it to be destroyed."[10] Still, Merton never let his dialogue with society on the topic of war and violence devolve into monologue. He made great strides to understand the contexts, histories, and internal logic of decision makers and situations. The openness he demonstrated in his approach to prayer and culture likewise was reflected in his engagement with society.

In the end, Merton occupied a position that advocated Christian nonviolence as the normative disposition in the face of conflict. He refrained from appropriating the moniker "pacifist," largely for fear that it was too often mistaken for "passivity." A nonviolent stance was anything but passive; it was a radical response that required imagination and creativity, true dialogue and compromise. He recognized that in the age of the overpowering military-industrial complex, the United States' default solution to domestic and international problems was nearly always military in nature.

His dialogue with society concerning war and violence also included a critical conversation with his own theological tradition. Merton was, in principle, an adherent of the ancient "just war" theory, which stated that given a number of specific criteria, it is conceivable that a violent response to a military aggressor can be justified. I say Merton was "in principle" in support of "just war" because he stated himself that, *in practice*, a justifiable war could not be conducted in the nuclear age.[11] The conversation in which Merton engaged was one that maintained a fierce loyalty to the Christian intellectual and moral tradition, but also did not shy away from challenging questions and propositions. Indeed, as Pope Francis observed, Merton was not at all afraid to challenge pre-conceptions or "certitudes" of his time—both within the Church and outside it.

Merton was also deeply concerned with the reality of racism and the struggle for civil rights underway in the 1960s, which he recognized as tied to the larger ill of American society—violence. He was closely attuned to the institutional and structural evils that perpetuate racial injustice, prejudice, and discrimination. Long before the technological revolution of smartphones and social media that have brought wider attention to systemic injustices, Merton understood that what was widely characterized by politicians and white-controlled media as isolated instances of violence in communities of predominantly persons of color was in fact symptomatic of a more insidious reality of institutional racism masked as "law and order." In an essay that begins with the line, "Theology today needs to focus carefully upon the crucial problem of violence," Merton writes: "Hence murder, mugging, rape, crime, corruption. But it must be remembered that the crime that breaks out of the ghetto is only the fruit of a greater and more pervasive violence: the injustice which forces people to live in the ghetto in the first place. The problem of violence, then, is not the problem of a few rioters and rebels, but the problem of a whole structure which is outwardly ordered and respectable, and inwardly ridden by psychopathic obsessions and delusions" (*FV*, 3).

Merton's dialogue with society on the topic of racism and civil rights took an optimistic look at Martin Luther King Jr. and the hope that Christian nonviolence would prevail. But by the mid-1960s, and then with King's assassination in 1968, Merton became disillusioned with the prospect that nonviolent action could work in his country. He never goes so far as to endorse violent action, but he does express a sort of solidarity and empathy with those women and men of color who might consider violent force as a means to overcoming racial injustice in the United States (*FV*, 121–29).

Merton's writings on race are simply astounding. What is most striking is his consistent and clear conviction that the problem of racism is not a black problem but *a white problem*. In his classic essay "Letters to a White Liberal," he offers a lengthy engagement with the signs of the times in the context of the struggle for American civil rights. His general thesis is that, while Congress passed the Civil Rights Act of 1964, there remains little beyond the written legislation to enact the desired intention of the law. Racism in the United States is so deeply imbedded in the culture and collective imagination that it will take much more than words on paper to change the status quo. In fact, Merton argues that the white Christian communities in the North (i.e., "white liberals"), which seem ostensibly supportive of civil rights, are in fact complicit in the subjugation of persons of color and the perpetuation of structural racism. They do not wish to surrender the society with which they are familiar, nor do they want to acknowledge and then give up the unearned privileges afforded them because of their skin color.

Often during the 1960s, Merton challenged his interlocutors, especially those who identified as Christian and white, to acknowledge their complicity. In another powerful essay, "The Hot Summer of Sixty-Seven," he writes:

> There is . . . such a thing as collective responsibility,
> and collective guilt. This is not quite the same as per-
> sonal responsibility and personal guilt, because it does
> not usually follow from a direct fully conscious act of
> choice. Few of us have actively and consciously *chosen*
> to oppress or mistreat the Negro. But nevertheless we
> have all more or less acquiesced in and consented to a
> state of affairs in which the Negro is treated unjustly,
> and in which his unjust treatment is directly or indi-
> rectly to the advantage of people like ourselves, peo-
> ple with whom we agree and collaborate, people with
> whom we are in fact identified. So that even if in theory
> the white man may believe himself to be well disposed
> toward the Negro—and never gets into a bind in which
> he proves himself to be otherwise—we all collectively
> contribute to a situation in which the Negro has to live
> and act as our inferior. (*FV*, 180)

The dialogue with society in this case starts with humility, as Merton acknowledges his own social location and his own identification—"we," "us," and "ourselves"—with those with whom he is engaging. Unless conscious, deliberate efforts to recognize and surrender white privilege, listen to those oppressed by racism, and then do something to change the status quo are deployed, nothing will change. And the fault rests with predominantly white, racist society, which does not exist apart from all those willfully ignorant individuals that compose it.

Merton's dialogue with society always began with his owning his own place within it. Although many were openly hostile and dismissive of his social criticism in the moment, the passage of time has only clarified his prophetic insight and prescience.

DIALOGUE WITH RELIGIONS

Pope Francis lauded Merton as a "promoter of peace between peoples and religions"—and, of all the forms of dialogue, it is precisely for ecumenical and interreligious dialogue that Merton is best known. As we have already seen, his starting point for engaging with other religious traditions was to situate himself securely in his own faith tradition: Roman Catholicism.

In a 1965 letter to a man named Marco Pallis, who had studied Tibetan Buddhism for many decades before Merton first became interested in Eastern thought, Merton affirms the importance of knowing and embracing one's own religious tradition before being able to engage in interreligious dialogue in any meaningful way: "I agree entirely that one must cling to one tradition and to its orthodoxy, at the risk of not understanding any tradition. One cannot supplement his own tradition with little borrowings here and there from other traditions. On the other hand, if one is genuinely living his own tradition, he is capable of seeing where other traditions say and attain the same thing, and where they are different" (*HGL*, 469). This is Merton's modus operandi. He is speaking from his own experience as one who was once naïve and hostile to non-Christian (and non-Catholic) religious traditions, prior to the late 1950s, when he began talking with ministers and students of other Christian denominations, including Baptist, Methodist, and Presbyterian churches.[12] As a result of his secure standing as a Catholic, Merton was genuinely open to the experiences and insights of others. He was able to write in 1966, "I will be a better Catholic, not if I can *refute* every shade of Protestantism, but I can affirm the truth in it and still go further" (*CGB*, 129).

What began as openness to other Christian traditions in the West expanded to include Eastern Orthodox communities, writings, spiritualities, and theologies.[13] Then, Merton's turning toward the East was not simply limited to Christian churches, but led to other faith and philosophical traditions including Buddhism, Hinduism, Islam, and Judaism. His groundedness in his own Roman Catholicism afforded him the freedom, humility, and openness to earnestly engage in dialogue with other religions.

The Chinese scholar John Wu once wrote to Merton, "You are so deeply Christian that you cannot help touching the vital springs of other religions."[14]

Contrary to some misguided views of Merton, it must be emphasized that he was never interested in, or considered, leaving the Catholic Church or his community of Trappist monks. Instead, his efforts to dialogue among Christians and other faiths anticipated and then fulfilled what the Second Vatican Council taught. He was ahead of his time and his church when it came to dialogue with other religions, just as he was with the universality of holiness and contemplation for all women and men, the importance of Christians engaging with culture, and the need for critical dialogue with society. If there was any doubt lingering among the naysayers as to his fitness to serve as an exemplar for Christian living in our age, the Holy Father Pope Francis put an end to that uncertainty.

But we might ask what resulted from Merton's engagement and dialogue with other religions. The answer is given to us by the monk himself in *The Asian Journal*, which chronicles the last months of his life while traveling to the Indian subcontinent and Southeast Asia. In a lecture given in Calcutta in October 1968, Merton hinted at what he had come to recognize as the deep interrelatedness all people share despite both real and perceived differences. He remarked that there are always people who dare to live on the margins and therefore see the world in a different way than those in the mainstream. Such people help point the way to a possibility of "communication on the deepest level": "[T]he deepest level of communication is not communication, but communion. It is wordless. It is beyond words, and it is beyond speech, and it is beyond concept. Not that we discover a new unity. We discover an older unity. My dear brothers [and sisters], we are already one. But we imagine that we are not. And what we have to recover is our original unity. What we have to be is what we are" (*AJ*, 308). Merton was motivated to dialogue with other religions because he recognized—guided by prayer and the Holy Spirit—that there is something profoundly unifying about our human condition. If we remain isolated monads of religions, separate and defensive, then we will never come close to encountering a kind of unity that is not novel or fleeting, but original and divinely established. As Merton said simply in *No Man Is an Island*, "This truth never becomes clear as long as we assume that each one of us, individually, is the center of the universe" (*NMI*, xx). True dialogue is only possible when humility and the recognition of interdependence flow into interreligious friendship and conversation.

CONCLUSION

Merton wrote in a 1966 letter: "To me it is enough to be united with people in love and in the Holy Spirit, as I am sure I am, and they are, in spite of the sometimes momentous institutional and doctrinal differences. But where there is a sincere desire for truth and real good will and genuine love, there God Himself will take care of the differences far better than any human or political ingenuity can" (*HGL*, 373). Unity among people and between humanity and God were the motivations for each dialogue in which he engaged. It is this quest for truth, goodwill, and genuine love that enabled him to fearlessly and courageously speak from his heart, finding commonalities and learning about others, as well as to encourage others to do likewise.

Dialogue is an extraordinarily human endeavor that involves vulnerability and openness and requires humility and listening. We must work to understand better our own cultural, social, and religious contexts in order to genuinely engage with others about their respective experiences, perspectives, beliefs, and history. But there is a risk. Dialogue can be unsettling or even scary. The messiness of human interaction and relationship is at the heart of all dialogue, which is why Merton explains that we cannot simply retreat to an intellectual or scholarly study, for such a detached approach forestalls the peacemaking and bridge building that come only through friendship. This is why he writes, "[A]s long as the dialogue proceeds merely between research scholars and concerns only the objective study of documents, it will lack its most essential dimension" (*MZM*, 209). That essential dimension is relationship, which Pope Francis clearly understands and models by his words and deeds in our time.

7.

How We Understand Our Sexual Lives

Kaya Oakes

> I am awakened, I am born again at the voice of this my Sister, sent to me from the depths of the divine fecundity.
>
> —Thomas Merton, "Hagia Sophia"

Summer in Kentucky is a live animal. At night it is riotous with katydids, the male stridulating his legs, the female chirping in response. Katydids use these sonic signals throughout evenings so humid the air feels solid. Crickets rasp their way through the nights simultaneously, scraping their wings against one another. The insects are mating, laying their eggs to hatch in the fall.

The first night I spend in Kentucky, I can barely sleep. A northern Californian to the core, I hopelessly await the cooling fog that envelops us and tames the most viciously hot day into submission. The Miwok, the first people in northern California, sang songs to the fog's sentience, sang to chase it away, and sang to call it in. In Kentucky summer, there is no fog. There are days when the sun is blotted behind clouds, but the temperature still hovers in the nineties. There are days when it is equally hot (100 degrees) and humid (100 percent), and at night you are lucky if it descends into the eighties. Air conditioners stay on twenty-four hours a day in most of the homes I walk by, my skin impregnated with sweat until it's a gelatinous sack, but in the guest wing of the retirement home for Ursuline sisters where I stay, finding the control knob proves elusive until three days before I leave. As soon as I discover it and crank the dial, my room enters subarctic temperatures, and in the mechanical sputter and hum the insect orgy is muted at last.

I'm in Kentucky for two weeks to teach the writing of spiritual autobiography to graduate students at Bellarmine University. And among the books I've assigned is Thomas Merton's *The Seven Storey Mountain*, a book I've taught with Catholic students, Protestants, Jews, Unitarians, Buddhists, Muslims, and Nones. Within a day or so of arriving, I'd seen the Merton archives, his work shirt and priestly stole glassed into the same cases that held copies of his books in dozens of languages. I'd been driven downtown to view the plaque at Fourth Street and Muhammad Ali Boulevard (formerly Walnut)—where in 1958 Merton awakened "from a dream of separateness"—and there I do what the modern pilgrim is required to do: snap photos of the plaque honoring Merton's epiphany on my iPhone, and post them on Facebook. Some twenty years after I first read his work, the Merton trail unfurls before me. But it's a trail that never leads me to the woman who changed Merton's life.

A week into my visit, I'm driven out to the Abbey of Gethsemani. It's once again muggy and rains violently for most of the drive. My guide, the theologian Greg Hillis, is a friend to many of the monks, most of them now elderly, several of whom knew Merton. Greg points out the Kentucky knobs, hobbit-like mounds of earth, vividly green in contrast to California's drought-parched landscape. As we drive through the tiny towns that surround the monastery, he nods toward the woods nearby and says, "and that's where Merton went to make out with M."

Women are barely present in *Seven Storey Mountain*—just the shadow of Merton's mother, who died young, and the Catholic social worker Baroness Catherine de Hueck, who got him interested in poverty—yet most of my students at Bellarmine that summer are women. At Gethsemani, the monk who greets us takes us into the cloister to view a tree I ask about, and Greg mumbles discreetly that women aren't usually allowed in the cloister—that, in fact, until fairly recently, there was a sign forbidding our entrance. Later I will see a couple of women working in the gift shop and one or two in the back of the church with the other laypeople during Compline, but for most of the day, as we walk the grounds with the Trappist who was a novice under Merton and eat lunch at Merton's hermitage with a couple of other Trappists who knew him, my female footsteps are in the minority.

And yet it was a woman who upended Merton's monastic vows, because his love for her was not chaste, but sexual. She exists mostly in shadows, elliptical, her letters burned, her name reduced to an initial in his journals. Apparently, she is still alive, and it's not difficult to discover her real name with some Google searching. But we will be as discreet as Merton was, and refer to her only as M.

—— —— —— —— —— —— —— —— —— —— ——

We have trouble with the sexuality of saints. Or perhaps it is the saints who have trouble with their own sexuality, which we witness through the fogged glass of years, through censored manuscripts, through segments erased in autobiographies. In Augustine's

Confessions, his separation from his unnamed concubine, the common-law wife he lived with for fifteen years who fathered his son, is movingly recounted in Book Six. But in her anonymity and likely illiteracy, she vanishes forever into history thereafter:

> Meanwhile my sins were being multiplied, and my concubine being torn from my side as a hindrance to my marriage, my heart which clave unto her was torn and wounded and bleeding. And she returned to Africa, vowing unto Thee never to know any other man, leaving with me my son by her. . . . Nor was that my wound cured, which had been made by the cutting away of the former, but after inflammation and most acute pain, it mortified, and my pains became less acute, but more desperate.[1]

Dorothy Day, who was among Merton's hundreds of correspondents, tells us more about Forster Batterham in one sentence of *The Long Loneliness* than Merton ever really reveals about M. in the journals. "The man I loved," Day writes, "with whom I entered into a common-law marriage, was an anarchist, an Englishman by descent, and a biologist."[2] But unlike Merton and M., Day and Batterham actually lived together "in the fullest sense of the phrase." She bore his child, and in the letters she wrote to him edited by Robert Ellsberg, she is explicit in her physical longing. In 1925, she wrote to Forster that "my desire for you is a painful rather than pleasurable emotion. It is a ravishing hunger which makes me want you more than anything in the world."[3] Day at that point was twenty-eight, still fairly young, but well on her way in her career as a journalist and activist, and at the beginning of her conversion to Catholicism.

Merton, on the other hand, was fifty-one when he met M., who was still in her early or mid-twenties. That much of an age difference would doubtless raise eyebrows today, but M.'s youth was a match for Merton's stunted sexuality. He had, after all, been a celibate monk for a quarter of a century. As a student at Cambridge in the early 1930s, Merton entered a world where "the Edwardian era lasted on in upper and upper-middle-class England," according to Michael Mott, and "there was a poorly lit area in which the code of the gentleman and the ways of the cad were sometimes hard for outsiders to distinguish." Merton was neither a gentleman nor a cad, but equal parts of each. When he did get into sexual relationships with girls, he had to be discreet, and as Mott says, Merton "was not, by nature, discreet."[4]

One of those Cambridge girls Merton discreetly had sex with became pregnant, and though the story is murky, it appears that she gave birth to the child, and that Merton left England soon after. This woman, too, is lost to history: the rumor that she was killed in the Blitz seems to be just a rumor, and when he made simple profession, Merton referred to her only as "the person mentioned in my letters." When *Seven Storey Mountain* was headed for publication, all mention of his transgression was stripped from the manuscript. The child would be in his or her eighties today. She, most likely, is dead, and has been rendered forever mute: her letters to Merton, if she wrote any, have gone undiscovered or, more likely, were destroyed. Merton had a habit of burning women's letters.

— — — — — — — — — — —

As I write this it is midwinter, which in northern California is gray. This year, it is also damp: the first real rains after several years of drought have left the ground soggy. When I walk on grass, my feet come away muddy. Buds have already begun to shoot from the plum trees, as they do every year in February. A man sits across the room from me, pecking at a laptop. Twenty years ago, we met. We lived together for seven years before we got married in a civil ceremony, years in which we did what people do when they fall in love and live together, living together in "every sense of the word," as Dorothy Day would put it.

Merton's sexuality and his longing for this shadowy woman do not negate my veneration of him as a writer and spiritual guide for religious wayfarers like myself. At his grave at Gethsemani, I stared for a long time at the AA coins, the plastic rosaries twined around the arms of the cross that marks his final rest, the holy cards left behind by pilgrims, and saw the Merton I first encountered: unreachable, like so many saints. His late-in-life sexual awakening knocks him off of whatever pedestal those who like their saints well scrubbed would put him on. It humanizes him. It makes him more like us.

I come from a generation of feminism that embraced sexuality as a positive part of being a woman. I developed a womanly body at a young age and have subsequently had no choice but to deal with it. But the sexuality of my body was easy to come to terms with in the context of my generation, which saw feminism as intersectional—a product not just of gender, but also of race and class—and saw sexuality as an important part of those intersections. This, incidentally, has not made it particularly easy to be Catholic, since Catholic teaching about the sexuality of women is almost exclusively linked to reproduction. A few years ago, I had to explain sex-positive feminism to a priest who is roughly my peer in age. He was befuddled by the notion of women taking pride in their sexuality, enjoying it, deriving pleasure from it. It wasn't something discussed in the community of men in which he lives.

When Merton met M. in 1966, sex was roiling all around them, with women liberated by the birth control pill, frankly sexual music blasting from radios, and new ideas about sex and marriage entering the national conversation. Helen Gurley Brown's *Sex and the Single Girl*, which encouraged women to have careers and multiple sexual relationships, was published in 1962. In his journals, however, Merton reels from his sexual attraction to M., who seems to have been fairly frank about her desire to take things all the way. Soon after the affair began in letters and phone calls and furtive meetings, their love, he wrote, "is the real root and ground of everything and this sexual love can only at best be a sign. Hence I will never touch her" (*LL*, 45). That vow did not last long.

Clerical celibacy, for some of my friends, has been freeing: they are able to love more people deeply when they let go of their sexuality. But for others, it becomes a cage. Certainly St. Augustine was miserable when he abandoned his concubine and was crabby in his years of celibacy, and Dorothy Day continued to write longingly to Batterham after they separated. Men and women still leave religious life when they meet someone and cannot reconcile desire and celibacy. A good friend recently lost both of his parents. His father had been a priest, his mother a nun, they met, and you should easily be able to fill in the rest of the story. He was the only child of their late discovery of one another.

The discovery of this initially censored part of Merton's life caused a minor sensation when the sixth volume of his journals was published in 1997. What is less discussed in the many pages written about Merton and M. is how young and frankly immature he sounds in what he wrote about her. Much of it is adolescent in tone and style. On April 27, 1966, he wrote that "once again it was clearer than ever that we are terribly in love, and it is the kind of love that can virtually tear you apart" (*LL*, 46). On May 2, he wrote that he was "not lonely for M. but in some strange way lonely with her" (*LL*, 48). On May 4, he wrote that "she has settled down to a sweet little girl happiness that completely disarms and ravishes me." On May 17, he wrote that "the trouble with me and M. is that it is not a game." On May 20, they "made love and love and love and love . . . we were getting rather sexy" (*LL*, 50, 62, 66). Merton clarifies near this juncture in the journals that they had not had sex per se, and in the copy I checked out from the library, someone penciled into the margin in all caps: TOO BAD FOR YOU.

This is a middle-aged man in thrall to a young woman, which may be responsible for the treacliness of some of Merton's prose about the relationship. But what we learn about M. from the journals isn't really about M.: it's about Merton. We know she is a nurse in training, that she has a fiancé in another city, that she's familiar with Merton's books when they first meet in the hospital, that she is "a talker." But about M.'s faith, or dreams, or hopes for her own future, much is vague at best. Merton circles around the idea of marrying her, which seems to have been as much his idea as hers, and would have been a way for him to have sex with her without further riling his conscience. She seems to have loved him, but without her version of the story, what sacrifices that love entailed for her emotionally and physically are unclear.

Because their relationship was so dependent on others—M. didn't have a car, and neither did Merton, so friends had to ferry them to various assignations—others must have weighed in on the relationship. Mott says that Merton's friends were by turns happy for him that he'd fallen in love and annoyed by his behavior. Merton and M. had an assignation in the office of one of his friends who was a psychologist. It was that day that drove Merton to his confessor because he had broken his vow; most likely, he and M. finally had sex. He mentions her nakedness, his longing for her body after this meeting. The psychologist friend was furious at Merton for looping him into the mess by proxy.

It didn't take long before Merton and M. were discovered by way of a Trappist listening in on one of their phone calls through the abbey switchboard. He had encouraged her to label her letters as "Conscience Matter" in order to avoid their being opened. Phone calls, however, were more likely to be overheard. Having sex in a friend's office, making out on abbey grounds, and asking friends to arrange meetings in restaurants and at the airport were also risky, and frankly, not very smart. But love and lust are not smart emotions. As with the first signs of spring after a long winter, rationality goes out the window when glory arrives.

━━ ━━ ━━ ━━ ━━ ━━ ━━ ━━ ━━ ━━ ━━

Merton, even across the decades, cannot be separated from the vows he took. He writes about his agonies over his decision to remain at Gethsemani over choosing a life with M., and after his relationship with her is exposed, he confesses, "I am known as a monk in love with a woman" (*LL*, 84).

If the Merton in the journals throughout the period of the affair can occasionally sound juvenile, the Merton in its aftermath steadily comes to terms with the sense of maturity that often follows a personal upheaval. M.'s greatest concern about their separation, he reflects, was that they would "gradually cease to believe that we are loved" (*LL*, 97). For Merton, orphaned young and cast into an itinerant life until he grounded himself at the monastery, the idea of his essential self as unlovable and unworthy of love haunts the early years of his writing. The love of God and Christ can seem incarnate only in the distant past and therefore abstract. In monastic communities, there is very little touching, and touching is sometimes explicitly forbidden; the only regular touch Merton received was when he was under medical care. M., as his nurse, was one of the few people to lay hands on him. A friend undergoing treatment for cancer recently told me a similar story; a single woman, she received touches only from doctors and nurses. The profound loneliness this created lessened her sense of self. Merton seems to have felt the same.

What M. gave Merton, both in words and physicality, was a sense of being loved. More significantly, she gave him a sense of being worthy of love. Late in August of 1966, after the abbot asked Merton to make a choice between M. and Gethsemani, their correspondence and contact begin to dwindle. Nonetheless, Merton wrote, "there is a certain fullness in my life now, even without her. Something that was never there before" (*LL*, 119). The autumnal turn of his life had begun. He chose his vows, but chose them with the knowledge that his sexuality was part of his full and authentic self. Merton became whole, perhaps for the first time in his life. He found consolation.

Two years later, he would be dead. M. discovered his death in a newspaper. What we know about her subsequent life is scant, mostly by her own design. She chose to vanish into ordinariness rather than write an exposé or hit the talk-show circuit, and, assuming she is still alive, whatever correspondence of Merton's she might still be holding on to remains unread by anyone other than her. In the age of exposé in which we live, M.'s silence seems radical. It is the silence of a woman making a choice.

What M. gave Merton was an end to fear. He no longer feared the destructive forces he had battled for most of his life: the fear of death, the Noonday Demon, the self-loathing so many writers walk with as a constant companion. To know that one is loved is an end to fear. For the religious person, the love of God is sometimes not enough; the love of other flawed and fragile human beings is ballast against our own frailty and fallibility. But we must first be loved before we can love. For readers, M. will always move in shadows, but for Merton, her physical presence in his life continued to make a difference even after they parted ways. Her gift to him was this: to enable this great and troubled man to "no longer fear the ardent and loving forces in myself" (*LL*, 304–5). He took that ability to love all the way to Bangkok, to sudden death alone in his hotel room, to a heart stopped from electric shock. Her love would be with him in that moment, too.

PART II

Life Lessons in the
Light of Merton

1.

On the Hundredth Anniversary of Thomas Merton's Birth

Bishop Robert Barron

I write these words on the one hundredth anniversary of the birth of Thomas Merton, one of the greatest spiritual writers of the twentieth century and a man who had a decisive influence on me and my vocation to the priesthood. I first encountered Merton's writing in a peculiar way. My brother and I were both working at a bookstore in the Chicago suburbs. One afternoon, he tossed me a tattered paperback with a torn cover that the manager had decided to discard. My brother said, "You might like this; it's written by a Trappist monk." I replied, with the blithe confidence of a sixteen-year-old, "I don't want to read a book by some Buddhist."

With exquisite sensitivity, he responded, "Trappists are Catholics, you idiot."

The book in question was *The Seven Storey Mountain*, Thomas Merton's passionate, articulate, smart, and deeply moving account of his journey from worldling to Trappist monk. Though much of the philosophy and theology was, at that time, over my head, I became completely caught up in the drama and romance of Merton's story, which is essentially the tale of how a man fell in love with God. The book is extraordinarily well written, funny, adventurous, and spiritually wise. In one of the blurbs written for the first edition, Fulton Sheen referred to it as a contemporary version of St. Augustine's *Confessions*, and it was fulsomely praised by both Evelyn Waugh and Graham Greene. Moreover, it contributed massively to the startling influx of young men into monasteries and religious communities across the United States in the postwar era.

I was so thrilled by my first encounter with Merton that I dove headlong into his body of writing. *The Sign of Jonas*, a journal that Merton kept in the years leading up to his priestly ordination, became a particular favorite. That work concludes with an essay called "Fire Watch: July 4, 1952," which Jacques Maritain referred to as the greatest piece of spiritual writing of the twentieth century. In this powerful meditation, Merton uses the mundane monastic task of walking through the monastery checking for fires as a metaphor for a Dantesque examination of the soul. *The Sign of Jonas* is marked by Merton's playful and ironic sense of humor, but it also gives evidence of the enormous range of his reading and intellectual interests. To devour that book as a nineteen-year-old, as I did, was to receive an unparalleled cultural education. For many people of my generation, Merton opened the door to the wealth of the Catholic spiritual tradition: I first learned about John of the Cross, Meister Eckhart, Teresa of Avila, Bernard of Clairvaux, Odo of Cluny, the Victorines, Origen, Thérèse of Lisieux, and Hans Urs von Balthasar from him.

Perhaps the central theme of all of Merton's writings is contemplation. What he stressed over and again in regard to this crucial practice is that it is not the exclusive preserve of spiritual athletes, but rather something that belongs to all the baptized and that stands at the heart of Christian life. For contemplation is, in his language, "to find the place in you where you are here and now being created by God." It is consciously to discover a new center in God and hence at the same time to discover the point of connection to everyone and everything else in the cosmos. Following the French spiritual masters, Merton called this *le point vierge*, the virginal point, or to put it in the language of the fourth gospel, "water bubbling up in you to eternal life." In his famous epiphanic experience at the corner of Fourth and Walnut Streets in downtown Louisville, Merton felt, through *le point vierge*, a connection to the ordinary passersby so powerful it compelled him to exclaim, "There is no way of telling people that they are all walking around shining like the sun" (*CGB*, 155).

Sadly, for many younger Catholics today, Merton, if he is known at all, is viewed with a certain suspicion, and this is for two reasons. First, when he was a man of fifty-one, he fell in love with a young nurse who cared for him after back surgery. Though it is almost certain that this was exclusively an affair of the heart, it was certainly, to say the very least, unseemly for a middle-aged monk and priest to have been so infatuated with a much younger woman. At the same time, Merton worked through this confusing period and returned to his vowed monastic life. And the journal that he kept during that year is so spiritually alert and illuminating that I often recommend it to brother priests who are wrestling with the promise of celibacy. To dismiss Merton out of hand because of this admittedly inappropriate relationship strikes me as disproportionate.

The second reason that some younger Catholics are wary of Merton is his interest, in the last roughly ten years of his life, in

Eastern religions, especially Buddhism. They see this as an indi-
cation of a religious relativism or a vague syncretism. Nothing
could be further from the truth. Merton was indeed fascinated by
the Eastern religions and felt that Christians could benefit from a
greater understanding of their theory and practice, but he never for
a moment felt that all religions were the same or that Christians
should move to some space "beyond" Christianity. In order to
verify this, all one has to do is read the prefaces to his major books
on Zen and Buddhism.

About ten years ago, I had the privilege of giving a retreat to
the monks at Merton's monastery of Gethsemani in Kentucky. Just
after the retreat ended, Merton's secretary, Brother Patrick Hart,
took me out in a jeep to see the hermitage that Merton occupied
the last few years of his life. While we were sitting on the front
porch of the small house, he looked at me intently and said,
"Could you tell anyone that's interested that Thomas Merton
died a monk of Gethsemani Abbey and a priest of the Catholic
Church?" He was as bothered as I am by the silly suggestion that
Merton, at the end of his life, was on the verge of leaving the
priesthood or abandoning the Catholic faith.

Thomas Merton was not perfect, and he might not have been
a saint. But he was indeed a master of the spiritual life, and his
life and work had a profound effect on me and an army of others
around the world. I offer this birthday tribute as a small token of
gratitude.

2.

How Thomas Merton and the Music of Keith Jarrett Changed My Life

KEVIN BURNS

I am a member of the analog generation that grew up assured that the word *friend* is a noun, not a verb. As a noun, a friend is someone we encounter and eventually learn to trust. As a verb, a friend is charged with the impossible: to guess the unspoken expectations that have been imposed on them. Not surprisingly, nouns linger as verbs seek their way to the exit.

I met him quite by chance in a bookstore in 1981. I was lost. I'd walked round and round the brick-built circular Catholic church that I could not bring myself to enter. I felt drawn to it, yet unable to reach for its wooden doors. Some unfinished Catholic business from the past was picking and poking away, again. Unsettled, I turned away, walking aimlessly. Down the street was a bookstore. This was a familiar door, easily opened. It was midafternoon, and there were not many customers. Breathing deeply, I browsed without purpose, trying to regain some composure. I stopped in front of the section marked "Religion." On the shelf at eye level was a homemade cardboard star with "New!" written in red marker. I reached for the book next to the star and started flipping through its pages without really focusing until these lines caught my attention: "While I am asking questions which You do not answer, You ask me a question which is so simple I cannot answer. I do not even understand the question" (*SOJ*, 353).

Time seemed to stop right there. Formulate your question before running off with raw uncooked answers to something you haven't fully assessed. Those simple words cut to the heart of the matter. But who was this author who had captured my attention with two sentences? Thomas Merton was the name on the cover. There was no photograph. I noted that "new" didn't mean recent, and that this was a new edition of a book initially published in 1953, when I was an infant. I bought the book, called *The Sign of Jonas*, and left for home. That evening, and well into the night, I read it in the company of someone else I had met quite by chance, Keith Jarrett. On the stereo, he was playing *The Köln Concert*, reassuring me in music that tensions, like questions, also seek and sometimes find fleeting resolution, like a writer's words on a page.

I realized I had jumped deep into the details of an unfolding story as Merton described his experiences of living in a Kentucky monastery. These were interesting fragments, but I had no context for them. Who was he, and how did he end up there? Then

I reached that great final chapter, "Fire Watch, July 4, 1952." It's elegant, crafted writing in a voice that moves with ease from detailed descriptive autobiographical narrative to what sounded to me like prayer. "There are drops of dew that show like sapphires in the grass as soon as the great sun appears, and leaves stir behind the hushed flight of an escaping dove" (*SOJ*, 362). This was writing from the familiar to the liminal and the numinous, and then back to the here and now.

I was confident that this author/monk could somehow help me to "understand the question"—especially when the soundtrack to his words was the beguiling harmonic reach and breathless melodic energy of Keith Jarrett. He captured so powerfully in sound what this author was crafting in words.

Twelve other books were listed in the preliminary pages of *The Sign of Jonas*. In those pre-Internet days, only a visit to a library could produce information that is a single keystroke away today. All the references pointed to Merton's *The Seven Storey Mountain* as essential reading. That's where I turned next.

> I stepped down out of the car into the empty night. The station was dark. There was a car standing there, but no man in sight. There was a road, and the shadow of a sort of a factory a little distance away, and a few houses under some trees. In one of them was a light. The train had hardly stopped to let me off, and immediately gathered its ponderous momentum once again and was gone around the bend with the flash of a red tail light, leaving me in the middle of the silence and the solitude of the Kentucky hills. (*SSM*, 350)

This uncertainty resonated with my tentative meandering up and down Catholic byways and dead ends. I knew from the *Jonas* book what happened when he found himself at this destination. For him to finally get there—and know where "there" really was—required him to address unfinished business from his younger years. The more I read about his struggles over direction and purpose in *The Seven Storey Mountain*, the more my own questions took shape. I was midway through that book when Monica Furlong's *Merton: A Biography* was released, and I was able to read two versions of a life story side by side. She focused on a Merton "with his fair share, perhaps more than his fair share, of human frailties."[1] He gave his frailties a purpose, describing them as the "confusion and fog [that] pile up in your life, and then by the power of the Cross things once again are clear, and you know more about your wretchedness and you are grateful for another miracle" (*SOJ*, 323–24).

Merton offered reassurance in print, suggesting words to apply to my questions. I sought out all the Merton books I could find. Then, in 1984, something important surfaced. Michael Mott's voluminous biography, *The Seven Mountains of Thomas Merton*, revealed the fifty-one-year-old Merton's intense feelings for his young nurse, a detail not included in Furlong's biography. He wrote: "Out of uniform, with her long black hair free except for a broad headband, she was more overwhelming than he had remembered. His resolution to talk to her, not to touch her, went for nothing."[2]

Merton suddenly became a very human wounded healer. The revelations continued in the volumes of letters and journals that appeared in the decades after Mott's biographical portrait. I followed this more complicated Merton as I followed each new release of my other virtual friend, Keith Jarrett, buying and devouring each new LP (in those days) as it appeared. I experienced their works as intertwined, each reflecting and adding new insights to the other: Merton's clarity with simple words for complex matters, filtered through Jarrett's elaborate abstractions of harmony, tension, dissonance, and those aching fleeting moments of release. These two American artists became (and continue to be) inseparable for me. And as with any true artist, they keep shifting their creative ground. Some works speak more directly and immediately than others, some mature slowly, offering deeper resonances each time you return to them. Others don't work and are best left off the playlist or reading list altogether, or until you are finally ready for them. Always, though, there is that one work you treasure above all the rest. For me it's Merton's *Jonas* book—with its coincidental yet essential soundtrack, Jarrett's *Köln Concert*—not because of the work itself, but because of all the enriching transformations it has led to.

I've now read all the published journals, letters, and books that Merton wrote in his interrupted life, and most of the works written about him. His toughness, humor, humility, and boundless curiosity continue to surprise, discomfort, and challenge. I am embarrassed by the imbalance, though—how little I can offer this virtual friend in return, except a determination to share my profound gratitude for his encouragement to keep digging for the right words for those important but elusive questions that all soul-seekers struggle with. In that initial encounter, he offered simple, life-changing verbs and nouns to work with. I use them still: "Questions arrive, assume their actuality, and also disappear. . . . There is greater comfort in the substance of silence than in the answer to a question. Eternity is in the present. Eternity is in the palm of the hand. Eternity is a seed of fire, whose sudden roots break barriers that keep my heart from being an abyss" (*SOJ*, 361).

3.

Anatomy of a Conversion

Paula Huston

Just last week during Thanksgiving dinner at our house, eaten outside in the sharp, rain-washed, brilliant air you can only find in California on a perfect fall day, I had a conversation with someone I barely know, a young man of thirty, a husband and father of two, handsome, out of work, very likely despairing but hiding it under a practiced if weary smile (years in the "hospitality industry," as he put it). The only thing I knew about him prior to our talk was that his three-year-old son and baby daughter had just been baptized into the Roman Catholic Church—this, despite his not being Catholic or even able to say whether he was a believer. I told him I found that both admirable and puzzling. Why had he agreed to do it? He admitted he never would have thought of it on his own—he'd been raised like most of his generation, without religion—but he himself had at least been baptized as an infant and it seemed important for him not to stand in the way of his wife's desire that their children should be too. "But the whole thing was nice," he assured me, still sounding surprised though the event had taken place some days ago. "Really nice. I'm glad I was there."

Nice, perhaps, but getting to this point could not have been easy for him. When he and his then-girlfriend began living together, she'd been far, far from the faith in which she'd grown up. But then they had married, had their son and daughter, and somewhere in the midst of becoming responsible for the formation of two young human beings, she'd rediscovered her Catholic roots. Now she went to Mass each Sunday and oftener if she could, taking their little son with her while her husband stayed home with the baby. I asked him if that was hard, having her so dramatically embrace this religion he knew almost nothing about. He admitted it was a bit scary at first—he wasn't sure what it all meant, and more importantly what it would mean for the two of them as a couple—but slowly he began to realize that what she had found was vastly superior to anything else on offer, at least anything he'd ever experienced. It lent meaning to her life, the kind of meaning he'd almost but not quite written off as illusory. He described the endemic rootlessness of the hospitality industry culture. It's so easy, he told me, to let your time slip by you. To think that drifting means you're free. And then one day you wake up and you're fifty and still waiting tables. No family, even if you used to want one. Nothing to look forward to except the next paycheck. So maybe you buy a new car. Or maybe you move to a new city. Maybe that'll help it all make sense.

For a moment we sat staring into the abyss together. Then he sighed, raking back his hair. "That could have been me. I was so lucky."

I nodded. It was true.

He gave me a grave, determined look. "So now that this has happened, I don't want to be left out. I don't want to be the dad who never goes to church with his kids. I need to learn about this stuff."

——— ——— ——— ——— ——— ——— ——— ——— ——— ——— ———

When I first read Thomas Merton's spiritual autobiography, *The Seven Storey Mountain*, I hadn't pondered the question of meaning since my early teens. And not because I'd been drifting, either. I'd been too busy getting married, having kids, getting a divorce, getting remarried, working on my degree, landing a job, getting a real career going at last. Now I was forty and, contrary to all my expectations—after all, look at how hard I'd worked to find happiness—I was suffering from a case of self-hatred so severe I could hardly look at myself in the mirror. More frightening even than this was the sense of futility that was dogging my days. What did it mean, all this effort and struggle? What was the point? And then one night I read Merton's account of the breakdown he went through while still in college: "I lay on the bed and listened to the blood pounding rapidly inside my head. I could hardly keep my eyes closed. Yet I did not want to open them, either. I was afraid that if I even looked at the window, the strange spinning inside my head would begin again. . . . And far, far away in my mind was a little, dry, mocking voice that said: 'What if you threw yourself out that window . . .'" (*SSM*, 179).

I recognized that voice I'd been hearing it too. The only thing saving me at this point was that I was too busy to stop and think clearly about what was happening to me. I was also too nervous; I was afraid that if I paid any sort of real attention to the question "What does it all mean?" I might not get up the next morning. But now I knew that I wasn't the only one this sort of psychological crisis had ever happened to, that in fact a famous monk had gone through it too, and this gave me the courage to peer into the unexplored depths of my predicament. In the process, I realized something that had never occurred to me before: that how my life was going to turn out was not in fact up to me. I'd thought that even during the most chaotic parts of it—the divorce, single motherhood, the many money problems—I was at the controls. That through sheer willpower, I could eventually make things go my way. By all appearances, I had—yet look at me now.

Merton's first important spiritual discovery was that all of it, whether drifting or striving, finally comes to the same place. We hedonists and romantics assume that if we can only keep clear of constraints, doing what feels good at the time, life will eventually bump our small coracle into some sweet, safe harbor. We workaholics white-knuckle our way through over-the-bow waves, fiercely convinced we know where we are going and why. And then one day we gaze over the side of our brave little craft into swirling fathoms of dark water, and the thought we've been counting on—that if only we hang in there long enough or work hard enough, we will arrive—gives way beneath us. For some of us, and Merton was one and so were Augustine and Tolstoy, it happens that fast. We have been brought face-to-face with the great question: What's it all about? And to realize we have no answer can feel like a violent and sickening blow. Merton says, "It was as if some center of balance within me had been unexpectedly removed, and as if I were about to plunge into a blind abyss of emptiness without end" (*SSM*, 178).

The terror this experience unleashes can overmaster us. Existential fear can swallow up whole generations and cultures, as it did twentieth-century America at the beginning of the modern era, the years during which Merton was coming to young manhood. And once dread has us—once we come to believe that there really is no inherent meaning to our lives, no transcendent point toward which we as an entire species are aimed, no Good, no True, no Beautiful—nothing solely human can defend us against the nightmare. This was Merton's second big spiritual discovery, and one that I was in the midst of ferreting out for myself when I first read these lines: "There is a paradox that lies at the very heart of human existence. It must be apprehended before any lasting happiness is possible in the soul of a man. The paradox is this: man's nature, by itself, can do little or nothing to settle his most important problems. If we follow nothing but our natures, our own philosophies, our own level of ethics, we will end up in hell" (*SSM*, 185). So *this* is where I was headed, or perhaps already was: in a hell of my own making. But how to save myself? How had Merton saved himself?

It seemed that he'd started listening to the second voice. For there were two inside him, just as there were two inside me, and they were at war. As long as he claimed sole authority over his life, the first voice, the mocking voice that filled him with dread, dominated his consciousness. Whenever he let down his guard, the other, quieter voice became audible, and it was telling him quite simply and clearly what he should do: go to church. Eventually, and despite much prevaricating and self-doubt and self-consciousness, he went to his first Mass, which had an immediate and, as it turned out, permanent effect on the course of his life. What was it that so impressed him? According to his memoir, it was the sight of so many people of all ages and types coming together as one, their attention directed not at themselves or each other but beyond, toward some great transcendent mystery that called forth awe and gratitude and humility in them. They had not succumbed to the darkness; for them, the darkness had been overcome. Merton says, "What a revelation it was, to discover so many ordinary people in a place together, more conscious of God than of one another: not there to show off their hats or their clothes, but to pray, or at least to fulfill a religious obligation, not a human one" (*SSM*, 227).

The homily that morning, the first he'd ever heard, reinforced these impressions: "How clear and solid the doctrine was: for behind those words you felt the full force not only of Scripture but of centuries of a unified and continuous and consistent tradition"

(*SSM*, 228). And the words themselves were more than simply words to this congregation; they were life-giving nourishment. This single experience of a Sunday morning spent differently than he usually would—sleeping in, reading the paper, having coffee with his girlfriend—was enough to break the grip of the specter: "I could not understand what it was that happened to make me so happy, why I was so much at peace, so content with life, for I was not yet used to the clean savor that comes with an actual grace. . . . All I knew was that I walked in a new world" (*SSM*, 230).

The *Seven Storey Mountain* was not the only reason I myself finally wound up at Mass and went on to become a Catholic, but it was immensely influential at a time when I needed to know I was not alone, that my psychological desperation was not personal or unique or rooted in my childhood but was instead the result of a full-blown spiritual crisis. And more, that there was a way to get through it, even to become a new kind of human being, if only I had the courage to enter the door of the Church.

━━　━━　━━　━━　━━　━━　━━　━━　━━　━━　━━

Everyone had left the table by now, carrying dishes and goblets and serving bowls with them as they went. We could hear water running in the kitchen sink, the clatter of silverware, laughter. The air was still bright though starting to cool, and the kids ran joyous and shrieking through the olive trees. Was there something wise I could say, something that would snap it all into focus for my new young friend the way Merton had helped snap it into focus for me? No, I didn't think so. Inside him, the two voices were already locked in mortal combat—I could hear this whether or not he could hear it yet himself—and it was clear he was starting to listen to the second of these, the revelatory, life-disrupting one, though who knew yet how it would all come out? As someone who understood a little about what he was going through, however, I could pray for him, and I would.

And then, at some point, one way or the other, just like Merton, just like me, he would have to make his choice.

4.
Conversion in Morningside Heights

Rabbi Phil Miller

In the fall of 1982, I arrived on the campus of Columbia University in New York City's Morningside Heights. I was an eager but scared eighteen-year-old freshman, just out of the womb of my mother's north New Jersey house and a heady, romantic senior year of high school. I did not realize this at the time, but as I turned the corner from 115th Street onto Broadway, I was taking the first steps toward a conversion—first, to the brink of baptism into the Catholic Church, and eventually, as a *ba'al t'shuvah*, returning to my birthright, Judaism. (I use the word "convert" to connote both one who is choosing a new religion and one who is a *ba'al t'shuvah*, experiencing spiritual transformation and returning to their birthright faith tradition.)

In the winter of 1935, Thomas Merton arrived in Morning-side Heights, also to attend Columbia University. His head was filled with "good resolutions . . . coinciding with a few superficial notions of Marxism" (*SSM*, 150). He too did not realize it at the time, but his emergence from the subway onto 116th Street and Broadway had brought him to "the shore at the foot of the high, seven-circled mountain of a Purgatory steeper and more arduous than I was able to imagine" (*SSM*, 242). This purgatory would be his conversion to the Catholic Church and a life as one of the century's greatest moral voices and poets.

There are mountains of literature on the elements of spiritual conversion. That study may be a mountain worth climbing. How-ever, I only wish to write a few words about the story Merton tells of his conversion in Morningside Heights. There, I first read *The Seven Storey Mountain* when I was stepping onto the shore at the foot of my own path to spiritual rebirth/*t'shuvah*. Pieces of Merton's story particularly spoke to me over thirty years ago, and still do today. Merton's book speaks to the universal human experience of conversion. It still serves as a guide to any human undergoing their own conversion within the habitation and name of their neighborhood, streets, and cities.

By mistake, or by the providential designs of God, Merton walked into Mark Van Doren's 1936 class on Shakespeare. This class was his most rewarding during his studies at Columbia. There was the content of Shakespeare's poetry itself. Books, both poetry and prose, are essential to any conversion experience. However, it was the teacher, Van Doren, through whom Merton learned "of the things that were really fundamental—life, death, time, love, sor-row, fear, wisdom, suffering, eternity" (*SSM*, 197). A convert needs a teacher who brings to life the words on a page. One of modern Jewry's great sages, Abraham Joshua Heschel, called on teachers to be "text people." They must live and model the moral and spiritual struggles and triumphs that underpin the sacred, classical texts they teach. The teacher also creates dialogue with these books. "All that year we were, in fact, talking about the deepest springs of human desire, hope and fear," Merton explains (*SSM*, 197). It is not impossible to tap these deep springs without a teacher. The teacher, however, is the "tender pioneer" that has walked through the mountains and valleys of these texts and has experienced their own conversion along that journey. It is the teacher sitting in *chevruta*/partnership with the student/convert that allows the texts to unlock the convert's own deepest wellsprings.

Not every convert shares a classroom with a Mark Van Doren or Daniel Walsh, another of Merton's Columbia teachers. The Talmud urges all potential converts and seekers to *aseh l'cha rav*, make for yourself a teacher. The commentaries question the use of the verb "to make." One commentary interprets this verb choice to mean that a person must actively search for teachers. We cannot wait for a Mark Van Doren to enter our lives. Rather, we must actively search but also accept whom we find as teachers, text people, and guides.

The second half of the Talmudic teaching to make for yourself a teacher is *kneh l'cha chaver*/acquire (literally, purchase) for yourself a friend. Here, too, the local habitation and names of Merton's story of his life at Columbia in Morningside Heights serve the convert. "God brought me and a half dozen others together at Columbia and made us friends, in such a way that our friendship would work powerfully to rescue us from the confusion and misery in which we had come to find ourselves" (*SSM*, 195). Later in life, Merton would seek the seclusion of the monastery. However, on the shore at the foot of the seven storey mountain, he needed friends. These friends did not all follow in his path. But they shattered his solitude cared for him, and supported him as he walked the shore and looked up at the mountain. Friends Ed Rice, Gerdy, Bob Lax, and Seymour, the last three all Jewish, walked with him up Broadway to church on the Sunday of his baptism, witnessed his immersion, and joined him for a meal afterwards in the rectory. "We all sat around the table and there was nothing incongruous about the happiness I then felt at all this gaiety . . . and certainly everybody was glad at what had been done" (*SSM*, 249). The Talmudic commentaries also question the verb choice for friendship; *acquire* a friend. Again, our commentator urges us to not passively wait for the perfect friend or soulmate. Rather, we must bond with the people in our lives who show us care and concern even, or especially, if they are on a different path than the one to our particular conversion. It is those friends, with their own names, idiosyncrasies, and narratives, who will stand with a convert as she steps onto the mountain.

The journey of conversion, of any spiritual transformation, runs through a sacred space. I found sacred space in Morningside Heights. First, I found it in St. Paul's Chapel on the Columbia campus at Father Paul Dinter's daily Mass at noon. Later, my journey took me to Shabbat morning prayer at the humble, book-filled apartment of Rabbi Eliezer Finkelstein at the corner of 106th Street and Riverside Drive. Merton found sacred space in the Church of Corpus Christi, "hidden behind Teachers College on 121st Street" (*SSM*, 226). He had been spending every Sunday with a young woman out on Long Island. However, "I was filled with a growing desire to stay in the city and go to some kind of church. . . . [T]here was the sweet, strong, gentle, clean urge in me which said: 'Go to Mass! Go to Mass!'" (*SSM*, 225–26). Sacred space can offer community, have ancient historical significance or aesthetic prowess. More than anything, it is where we experience God's presence most intimately. *Ta'amu u'rauh kee tov Ha Shem*: Taste and see that the Lord is good (Ps 34:9).

Merton's first entrance to Corpus Christi was tentative and ambivalent. He sought a place in the pews that he hoped would be obscure. However, he found it a revelation that so many people were "more conscious of God than of each other" (*SSM*, 227). In the months ahead, Merton grew more comfortable praying and encountering God's presence in Corpus Christi. It was there that he met another teacher, Father Moore, who would baptize him, and Father McGough, who would hear his first confession. All the world is God's indeed, but that is from God's perspective. Merton, like any convert, needed a particular space that he could return to regularly—not just to know God was in his world but also to know sensually, extraordinarily, that God was in this place and in his life.

Merton made many decisions and took great initiative toward his conversion. Nevertheless, throughout his narrative he shows keen awareness of what Jewish tradition more comfortably calls *yad Ha Shem*/the hand of God and what many Christians call grace. Shortly after arriving in New York City, "I happened to have five or ten dollars burning a hole in my pocket. I was on Fifth Avenue for some reason or other and was attracted by the window of Scribner's bookstore, all full of bright, new books." He walked inside and picked up a book by Étienne Gilson. The book and Gilson would have a profound influence on Merton throughout his life. It was "real grace" that had brought him to Fifth Avenue and to stop and look in the window at Scribner's. It was grace that would bring him to Mark Van Doren. It was grace that would bring him to his friends, and it was grace that would bring him to Corpus Christi, conversion, and beyond. It can be a tremendous lifting of a burden to a convert to know that their striving will be met with grace. Grace will bless them with what seem like coincidences when they are least expecting it.

It was grace that brought Thomas Merton to the local habitations named Morningside Heights and Gethsemani Abbey in Kentucky. And it was grace that guided him to write his life story and his poems, which would inspire converts in so many places for so many years to come.

5.

Merton's Death as Seen from the Home Grounds

Br. Paul Quenon, O.C.S.O.

My first inkling that Father Louis was going to Asia was on the day of my solemn vows in June of 1968. As I was sitting on the lawn with my mother and some other family members after the ceremony, he stopped by and invited me to come out to the lake that afternoon. He said that Bob Lax, his poet friend from Columbia University, and some other people would be there. It had been a hard, long six years following the novitiate, and it was a surprise and pleasure to receive this invitation from Father Louis. I had read Lax's new poetry volume, *The Circus of the Sun*. I wanted to see for myself if his face fit the description Merton gave: "face of a horse." It did. Another of these visitors was Richard Sisto, a young jazz musician from Chicago who ten years later would reconnect and

125

become my abiding friend. Another was Father Vernon Robertson, an Episcopalian priest who eventually became Catholic.

"Lax," as Father Louis always called him, sat with his gangly legs wrapped around the legs of a chair and poked holes in what Father Louis said. Father Louis would glow with an amused look as at an old game they played. Sisto's wife, a striking actress, recounted an incident of the night before when her husband was playing a drum. A moth was flying around a lighted candle, and just at the final slap on the drum, the moth flew into the flame. This became a significant story for me ten years later. One morning I was meditating before a candle when a moth began fluttering around it, and I was reminded of this story. Later that day, Richard showed up at the monastery, and by chance the guestmaster picked me to meet with him for a conversation.

By the lake, the conversation eventually turned to Buddhism, when Father Louis dropped a hint. He complained it was not enough to read what was written by Westerners to understand Buddhists. "I want to go and gain direct experience and talk with Buddhist masters myself." I was not surprised. Years previously, as his novice, I had a feeling he should go to Japan and encounter Zen Buddhism, his chief interest. I told him he ought to go there—as if I had some say in the matter. It was just an intuition. Perhaps it was in that same conversation, sitting across his desk in the novice master's office, that I expressed my feeling that "when you die your spirit will go ranging over the world." He slightly tilted his head back and breathed out, "Yeaaahh."

This, of course, was the summer of his trip to Asia, and he already had premonitions that he would die there. He told the abbot, Father Flavian, before he left that he might not come home alive. He said something similar to Dan Walsh, his teacher and friend at Columbia, who had moved to Gethsemani and become my teacher and that of others who had need or interest in philosophy. Father Louis dropped other hints, indirectly, during conferences with the novices and junior professed. For example, when one close friend of his died in a house fire, he spoke of how a person might have a sense of the arc of his life and of when it is rising and when it is descending. He made other off-hand quips such as, "I don't care what you guys do with monastic reform; I'm going to be out there pushing up the daisies."

As for me, a strange image flashed through my mind on the Solemnity of the Assumption, as I sat outdoors meditating, facing the woods of the hermitage. I imagined disappearing into the clouds above, wearing a pair of work boots such as Father Louis wore. That earthy quality made me certain it was about him. Just a curious image, that's all.

Eventually, I learned of his forthcoming trip to Asia thanks to Father Matthew Kelty, my confessor, and Father John Eudes, my spiritual director. Father Matthew served as Father Louis's confessor as well, and when telling me the news, he tilted his head, assuming Father Louis's lilting voice: "I'm going to Asia . . . I'm going to see the Dalai Lama . . . he reads my books!"

On the day of the big departure, Father Matthew waited out on the bank beside the highway in hopes of saying goodbye. He had received his own novitiate training, in the same years as I had, under the care of Father Louis. These two priests were peers, both born in 1915. I always knew when Matthew was receiving spiritual direction from Father Louis because there would be an uproar of laughter coming out the window. A personal farewell was much in order for Father Matthew. Unfortunately, he arrived too late to meet the car, and finally rose to return to the monastery. On the way Father Matthew broke out in tears with the realization that "we will never see Father Louis again." His Irish intuition proved all too true. That afternoon he bid Brother Lavrans, our iconographer, to draw a hand with a diamond in it. That evening Matthew showed the image to the class of juniors lately placed under his spiritual care. He told them, "Father Louis is our most precious gift in the monastery and we are about to lose him."

I likewise never found a chance to say goodbye. But a final image of Father Louis remains fixed in my mind. I was seated high on the balcony of the library when at a distance he emerged from the exit door of the ground tunnel, turned his back, and walked toward the hermitage. That somehow spoke to me, at that moment, as a definitive vision—his back turned, his head strong with intention, his steady stride away—and I did not like it, did not want to harbor the thought that this was the last sight. I tried not to believe that.

When I did hear, for certain, of his departure, I hurried on foot up to his vacated hermitage and sat on the floor of the porch, leaning my back against the front wall. All this seemed to build up to a huge moment. I tried to measure the meaning of this change for him and for the monastery. My imagination grew crowded with an image of Buddhist monks strolling up the lawn in front of me and entering the hermitage. I shied away from allowing such grandiose thoughts, but after many years I see I was not grand enough. The reality has happened over and again, including a visit by the Dalai Lama in 1996. But Father Louis would not be there to receive any of them—in the body at least.

As weeks passed, Father Louis mailed back brief items of news of the progress of his journey. The monastic conference in Thailand, of course, was to be the climax of the trip. The day came and went, with us waking in our own time zone. I never heard a thing until the community was seated at its midday meal and something unusual happened. After dinner was finished, Father Flavian walked to the reader's microphone—something he had never done before. He announced that a message had arrived that Father Louis had had an accident and was dead. Details were unclear because telephone service was inadequate. No further information was available, even the nature of the accident.

I immediately remembered how Father Louis once told our novitiate class that when he died, "I'll need you to say a lot of '*De Profundis*'s'" for me" ("Out of the depths . . ."). That is Psalm 130, one of the seven penitential psalms. I left the refectory, walked in a daze to the church, knelt, and said all seven penitential psalms—said them with intensity such as I had never done before, or since.

I wandered into the scriptorium to finish the interval where the choir monks were at their quiet reading. It was located above the boiler room, and at rare moments a safety pipe outside the window would release a buildup of excess steam. As I entered the room it roared out a white cloud of steam, and immediately I had the thought of how Jesus exhaled his last breath with a loud cry, bowed his head, and gave up his spirit.

That evening, after Compline, I entered the darkened scriptorium. Standing in the same spot, I noticed a holy card someone had left on the table. I picked it up and dimly saw, in Father Louis's handwriting, "*Charitas non deficit*"—love never falls away. It hit me directly like a punch in the chest. Like a message sent straight to my heart from an invisible hand. It was St. Paul's words, but it was Father Louis's message.

After that, time seemed to stand still. And time stayed that way. I spent a day and a night at Father Flavian's hermitage, settling into this new state of affairs. The stasis lingered for a week until the remains arrived from Thailand. It was much like the time after President Kennedy was assassinated—time stood still. That week seemed to drag out forever. The funeral itself began after a long wait as the casket was delayed at the undertaker's. Time weighed heavily.

The abbot had met with the coroner at the nearby Greenwell's Funeral Home in New Haven, together with Father John Eudes Bamberger, Brother Clement, and Mr. P. D. Johnson, a neighbor and friend of Brother Clement. I have learned through P. D.'s son, Fenton Johnson, that when they began to open the body bag for a viewing, the stench from the unembalmed body was so acute that they stopped and sealed it up again. That must have been a keenly penetrating moment for Father Flavian. When I saw him at Mass his skin was *pink*. All that, and the fact he had lost what he expected was the pillar of his future as a new abbot. Never before had I seen anyone's skin turn pink! He was normally pale-skinned, but this was an unnatural color. I never again saw it on him or on anyone else.

The casket rested before the sanctuary step and remained closed. The selection for the entrance chant at Mass was an old English hymn, "Now Praise We Great and Famous Men." Father Chrysognous, our organist, asked me, in preparation, to revise the words; so I changed it to "great and worthy men." I did not think Father Louis would be keen on being celebrated for his fame, especially at a liturgy. It is notable that this was the first time in memory that a change was made in the seating arrangement for guests. Both men and women were allowed on the ground floor of the church instead of attending from up in the tribune. It seemed much in character with Father Louis that such a change was effected. What added to the drama was that these guests were well-known publishers and writers and friends.

When the opening procession of concelebrants began, everyone behind and before me began to sing, and the long-awaited moment was too much for me. I broke into tears, trying to sing as best I could through it all.

Later, at the Offertory, standing to the side singing with the schola, I observed how the smooth, gray, slope-topped coffin nosed the sanctuary step, and it was a small, gray whale with Jonah inside—Father Louis swallowed up and brought back from across the world. And what sign might this prove to be? A sign for now, I asked, and for the future?

After Communion, when everyone was seated, a passage was read from the end of *The Seven Storey Mountain*. It was a brilliant choice for the occasion and seemed a synopsis of Father Louis's life, strangely defined even down to the present moment. At the end came these words as if spoken by the Lord about bringing him to the Cistercian abbey of the poor men who labor in Gethsemani: "That you may be the brother of God and learn to know the Christ of the burnt men" (*SSM*, 462). It sounded like a prediction of the manner of his death—"burnt," but with an electrical burn, and returned to the community "of the burnt men." Recently I found a clue to what Father Louis might have meant by that expression. It echoes the ending of his letter to Dom Frederic, his first abbot, in which he gives a summary of his life, much in line with the story of *Seven Storey Mountain*. He ends the letter with these words: "I came to Gethsemani December 10, and was admitted to the community on the Feast of St. Lucy, December 13; and now with many prayers and thanks to Almighty God I beg Him to make me, the least of all His servants, totally His so that my past life of rebellious sins and ingratitude may be burnt away in the fire of His infinite love" (*SOC*, 7). There were some auspicious facts that were already circulating in the community: Brother Patrick Hart told me Merton died on the same day of the year that he entered the monastery, December 10, and what is more, that he entered at age twenty-seven and died twenty-seven years later. To clinch the enigma, he died on the birthday of Dom James, his abbot of eighteen years.

The coffin stood by the graveside as light rain fell, and final prayers were said. Father John Eudes Bamberger was positioned at the head of the coffin. As it was about to be lowered, he put his hand to his lips and touched his hand to the coffin. Then the coffin was lowered, and the signal was given for a token number of shovels of dirt to be thrown in. Father Raymond, a vigorous man and Merton's monastic senior, was given the shovel. He labored with such gusto that the abbot had to touch his arm to stop him. As he was a writer himself, some may have seen that action as reflecting his rivalry in ambition and opinion. I saw it as rough Trappist realism about death and as reflecting years of comradery.

After the community departed, I climbed a ladder to retrieve a loudspeaker I had placed there, necessary to assist Father Flavian's soft voice. It hung in a red cedar, and as I climbed in the soft rain and placed my arms around the trunk the smell of cedar wood sweetened the sadness of the moment.

—— —— —— —— —— —— —— —— —— —— ——

Ten years later to the day, there was a memorial service with some Merton followers and neighbors. This was the first of several such services over the coming years. Brother Frederic Collins formed a Merton group, with myself and Father Michael Cassagram, which met every month. Richard Sisto had returned and moved into the neighborhood, on a property abutting our own, and his friend Father Vernon Robinson agreed to say Mass for our group in the guest chapel. Richard played the vibes, I did some singing, and Penny Sisto read some poetry. I took a notion to have a flame on the altar as a paschal motif. I found a beautiful ceramic bowl, filled it with lamp oil, and fixed a wick. All went well until the Sanctus. Just as Father Vernon reached the words "Blessed is he who comes in the name of the Lord," the bowl loudly exploded. Shards scattered all over the altar and the floor. Only a small flicker remained on the ceramic pedestal. Father Vernon, in his completely sedate manner, uttered, "Perfect timing!"

The explosion must have come because the flame had begun to diminish and the cooling of the bowl made it shatter loudly. You could credit that to my ignorance of ceramics, or credit Merton for sending a sign. A rather ambiguous one, as you might expect.

6.

The Restless,
Furious, Quietly
Abiding Friend
of Us All

Pico Iyer

A Hindu-born son of Theosophists, allergic to crosses and chapels after too many years of Anglican schooling—and, even more, someone based for thirty years in profoundly Buddhist Japan—I seem the last person who should be claiming Thomas Merton as my better self, my lifelong friend, the secret confessor who can feel at times like a ragged saint, precisely because he's so luminously human. And yet speaking directly, intimately, to someone like me, across every border, is exactly the grace the Cistercian monk offers to every age and continent. He makes exploration seem the calling of every honest soul, especially for those who refuse to give up on hope. He calls us to acknowledge what is deepest and most mysterious in all of us, even as he reminds us that we can't disappear into a cloud of piety, above it all. And he makes even the sometime absence of God a reminder of how much we feel the ache, and long for something truer than ourselves.

I knew next to nothing about Merton the first time I stepped into a Benedictine hermitage, on retreat, at the age of thirty-four, trying to ignore all the lecterns and the Bibles. I'd brought along my regular counselors, Emerson and Thoreau and even Oscar Wilde, to lead me into the beauties of aloneness. But then something unexpected began to happen. My little anxieties, my plans, my ambitions—almost everything I understood by my "self"— began to fade away in the silence, and I was enfolded in a reality as vast and still as all creation. Emerson and Thoreau told me of the depths I'd found in solitude, but I hungered for something to explain what this radiance meant and who I was when I wasn't an "I" I recognized.

So I walked up to the monastery bookstore and was directed toward a copy of *The Seven Storey Mountain*. The book looked promising; its author was a student of literature and almost as mongrel as myself. But as I went through the heavy volume in my cell, I found myself left behind by the young writer's certainties, the coup de foudre that had turned around his life and left him in love with a single way and life. In a curious way, the book lacked struggle, questioning, a sense that a life in a cloister can be as broken and harrowed as any life in the world—if only because a life in a cloister teaches one to look beyond distinctions between monastery and world.

So I put Merton on the shelf where C. S. Lewis sits—a great spirit and presence, but not one whose religious convictions spoke to me. Yet as I found myself drawn back into the silence, again and again, I started approaching Merton through the back door, as it were. A friend pointed me toward the "Fire Watch" section at the end of *The Sign of Jonas*, and I was transfixed—and not only because my own house had burned down a year before I first visited the hermitage. The Buddha himself would have embraced the white-robed father who saw that the world and all that's in it is a burning house, and "everything must burn."

I started reading the section called "Day unto Day," and began seeing how a life of obedience could bring its own kind of freedoms, even if they were always hard-won and sometimes hard to discern. I got a copy of *The Thomas Merton Reader* and started dipping into it as my daily grace, my lectio divina. I discovered the journals and the letters and a quality of honesty in restlessness, a refusal to assume that anything was completed or accomplished, that gave a life of holiness the cracks and open spaces I felt it needed. Today, as I prepare to lead a workshop at the oldest Zen monastery in the West next summer—just as when I was leading twenty-five dancers, rock 'n' roll musicians, and artists in discussions in Banff last month—my main text will be Thomas Merton.

Words and ideas, I sometimes feel, were Merton's perpetual nemeses. His busy mind was what kept him from the simple devoutness that was so often his great longing; it also led him into a busy life of distractions and new interests and projects and requests that left even his hermitage, by the sound of it, too cluttered. But for those of us outside the cloister, it was his ability to give voice to the love affair that is unsparing devotion that is his greatest offering.

Of course Merton is the spokesman of doubt, and doubt—the lonely night, the frustration of living in community, the days when Love is absent—is the very cornerstone of faith. Of course Merton is the great voice of questioning, wandering out into the world, into the silence of Zen, into poetry and politics, telling Henry Miller (in the glorious letters I discovered last year) that Miller's is the life he could have led—and, in his way, did live, perhaps. And of course Merton's is the voice of humanity, especially when, in his fifties, he fell desperately in love with a young nurse and started to question (again) much of what he had chosen.

As I began to guide my life by Merton's wavering flashlight, kind friends suggested that maybe it was his English boarding-school education, his time at Oxbridge, his love of poetry, his epiphany in Cuba that brought him close to me (since I shared all of these). But that is like saying that one chooses an honorary brother for the color of his shirt. The beauty of Merton is that he shed his circumstances at every turn, as much as he could, and had so many selves inside him that you could not begin to say he was one thing or the other.

By now, it's hard for me to see how I could have led my life without Merton under my skin, and circulating through my system. I grew close to the great singer-poet Leonard Cohen, an ordained Zen monk for five and a half years, and I found much of what he said and wrote, word for word, in Merton; the grace of the monastic calling is that it brings you, at moments, to a place where personalities become immaterial. Every monk writes with the ageless, planetary clarity of Anonymous. I fashioned a book of mine around Merton's *Asian Journal* and loved the way that, the deeper he traveled in Gethsemani, the more he pursued a truly catholic line of inquiry into every serious tradition.

I've spent much of my life circling around Graham Greene, and, of course, like Cohen, he shares a lot with Merton, in itchiness and complication and a faith so honest and self-questioning that it sometimes seems almost sub rosa. But Merton's strength is to know God's world and Caesar's world inside out, and to see how an acquaintance with each can deepen one's intimacy with the other. He confesses to all the vulnerability, the human frailty one finds in Greene, and yet he never loses a sense of what lies behind it, and who he might be if he got rid of a "he" entirely.

As I prepare to celebrate my sixtieth birthday, I realize that there've been just a handful of figures, all conflicted and wise, worldly and very much not who have felt as close to me as my own deepest intuitions, and closer than almost any family or friends. And Merton, so ready to lay himself open, to acknowledge all that he'd rather not acknowledge, to share every tremor of enthusiasm, delight, ambivalence, and occasional silliness (the word "silly," recall, comes from the Old English word for "blessed"), sits close to the heart of everything. Rarely a week goes by without my picking him up again, and finding myself called back to my deeper, truer self, even as my less true self is never wished out of existence.

Merton was a bridge in that regard—in many regards—whose fallenness gives us heart; he performed the great and liberating task of bringing hope and realism together. He was never other than a man, and yet he showed us how a man could be part of something vaster and less temporary.

Perhaps it's fitting—Merton would rejoice, I think—that Merton regularly comes back to me through his friend and public champion, the XIVth Dalai Lama. I've been visiting the Tibetan leader in his home in Dharamsala since 1974—six years after Merton visited—and I travel almost every November across Japan with His Holiness.

Over and over, the Dalai Lama recalls his Catholic friend as someone who taught him one of the most important lessons in a traveling life spent almost entirely in non-Buddhist countries. Over and over, he invokes Merton as someone who stands for exactly the kind of universal ethics—of attention and kindness and responsibility—he wishes to pass on. Like Merton, His Holiness knows and often says that the only way to change the world is to change the thoughts and desires of those who live in it. Like Merton, the leader of the Tibetans constantly reminds us that it is in helping someone else that we find the best way to bear our own trouble.

The last time I saw His Holiness, he told me how, growing up in isolated Lhasa, he thought that Buddhism was the greatest religion on earth. He'd barely seen another. Then, relatively soon after going into exile, he was visited by a Christian brother from Kentucky and saw that this man's devotion, clarity, and commitment to reality and potential was no less great, and that Catholicism had its own singular beauty and strength. For many, this course would be a more fitting one than Buddhism.

Merton has kept generations of Catholics honest, on their toes, and engaged (in every sense); one of the largely inadvertent graces of his journals is to show us how deeply patient and forbearing his abbots, and some of his fellow monks, must have been, to live with such an explosive in their midst. But what he does so beautifully for the rest of us—partly by intuiting the global order long before it was a reality—is to bring a tradition that many of us didn't know enough about very close, and to show us that it is not so far from what all of us hear in our most private hours.

Until I read Merton, I had a narrow, half-blind sense of what the Catholic tradition meant, and boxed it into stereotypes and prejudices of my own, mistaking the trappings for the soul. He brought it out into the daylight of the larger world by living it so intensely from within. Nowadays, when I visit his little private hermitage in Gethsemani, accompanied by a monk who studied under him, I can't deny the sense that I'm coming home. Thomas Merton gave many of us, from every tradition, a home, and he made it seem as large and timeless as the universe—and as familiar as the uncertain, often-anguished, always-yearning heart right here.

7.

Thomas Merton and the Realization of Us

Sylvia Boorstein

Back in the years when the question, "What book would you take with you to a desert island if you could take one?" made sense, I would respond, "Thomas Merton's *The Asian Journal*, specifically page 143." The entire book delighted me, perhaps because I felt it mirrored the situation I felt myself in at that time as a Jew—delighted to feel more connected to Judaism as a religious path than I had been as a child or even a young adult, and also a fairly well-known contemporary teacher of Vipassana (Mindfulness) meditation and the philosophy of the Buddha. I was accustomed to answering questions about being "both a Jew and a Buddhist" and glad to have Merton answering that same question from the perspective of a Catholic monastic.

Here is the specific part of Merton's *Asian Journal* I refer to above, the description of the day he spent with Chatral Rinpoche, a Tibetan Buddhist monk:

> We had a fine talk and all through it Jimpa, the interpreter, laughed and said several times, "These are hermit questions . . . this is another hermit question." We started talking about dzogchen and Nyingmapa meditation and "direct realization" and soon saw that we agreed very well. We must have talked for two hours or more, covering all sorts of ground, mostly around about the idea of dzogchen, but also taking in some points of Christian doctrine compared with Buddhist: dharmakaya . . . the Risen Christ, suffering, compassion for all creatures, motives for "helping others,"— but all leading back to dzogchen, the ultimate emptiness, the unity of shunyata and karuna, going "beyond the dharmakaya" and "beyond God" to the ultimate perfect emptiness. He said he had meditated in solitude for thirty years or more and had not attained to perfect emptiness and I said I hadn't either. . . .
>
> He told me, seriously, that perhaps he and I would attain to perfect Buddhahood in our next lives, perhaps even in this life, and the parting note was a kind of compact that we would both do our best to make it in this life. (*AJ*, 143–44)

My paperback version falls open easily to page 143 because I've gone back to look at it so often—to show my friends, to read it to students, to remind myself of this extraordinary conversation in which two modern-era men from vastly disparate cultures speak to each other so directly about their most intimate intimations of the divine and their respective ardency to establish that experience enduringly.

As I wrote that last sentence, I felt the same pleasure in my mind that I had when I first read about their encounter. I believe I recognize the state of absolute peace I think they both are pointing to. There have been times like that for me, in my own practice of Vipassana. I believe that these moments of impersonal awareness of the sublime source of creation behind the manifest world are rare in daily life, but not uncommon for people who have a strong and committed meditation practice, one that includes focused concentration along with awareness that is keen enough to dispel the sense of separateness that is our workaday consciousness. When the mind is still enough, duality disappears. and even if the experience is only momentary, it reorganizes the mind. Merton describes such an experience in *The Asian Journal* with the words, "everything is empty and everything is compassion" (*AJ*, 235).

It is only in recent years that I read Merton's description of crossing the street at Fourth and Walnut in Louisville, Kentucky, and feeling "as if waking from a dream, the dream of my separateness, of the 'special' vocation to be different . . . [and in that realization] . . . I too, became a member of the Human Race!" (*CGB*, 155).

In my own experience, my own discoveries of what the Buddha called "non-self" or "selflessness" were. for some years, limited to being amazed to find that—although it certainly felt as if there were some *one*, *me*, who was the owner of my experience, the seer, the hearer, the thinker, as well as the rememberer of it all—actually the sense of a separate subject of experience is illusory. The insight that the Buddha called "*anatta*" was in response to the Brahman concept of an enduring soul, Atman, and was meant to be a reformation of the religious understanding of his time. The definition of *anatta* as "emptiness" specifically means "empty of separations, interconnectedness of all being." I did not understand, for some years, how the realization that there was, after all, no enduring "I" supervising my life would transform my character. I now know that it did, though, in that way that Merton summarizes: "I became a member of the human race." To the degree that I am clear that my (and everyone else's) actions unfold according to habits developed by genetics, parenting, life experiences, by everything that produces an adult, I cannot construct victims or villains. There is no "one" to blame. I can, however, focus on the immeasurable suffering that is inevitably part of life, everyone's life unfolding and meeting challenges as best it can, and feel compassion.

I am writing this reflection in the middle of the Days of Awe, the first ten days of the Jewish New Year, 5777. One of the practices for this period of the year is the daily recitation of Psalm 27, which includes the verse: "One thing have I desired of the LORD, that will I seek after; that I may behold the beauty of the LORD and that I may dwell in the house of the LORD all the days of my life."

My sense of what dwelling in the house of the Lord would feel like is that there would be no "me" there, only "us," surrounded by compassion.

8.

Merton on the Spiritual Promise of Interreligious Dialogue

Acharya Judith Simmer-Brown

> I am convinced that communication in depth, across the lines that have hitherto divided religious and monastic traditions, is now not only possible and desirable, but most important for the destinies of Twentieth-Century [Hu]man[s]. (*AJ*, 313)

Through my decades of Tibetan Buddhist meditation practice and interreligious dialogue experience, I have often contemplated an encounter that took place in a bar in the Central Hotel in Calcutta, India, on October 19, 1963. It was the encounter between Thomas Merton in the last year of his life and my Tibetan Buddhist teacher,

Chögyam Trungpa Rinpoche, early in his teaching career in the West. This encounter, a fresh mutual inquiry about the spiritual life, has deeply influenced my life of dialogue and meditation practice.

Thomas Merton, known to his Trappist brothers as Father Louis, was fifty-three years old when he stepped off the plane in Calcutta for his much-anticipated Asian journey. Excited and jet-lagged, he met the twenty-eight-year-old Tibetan monk Chögyam Trungpa, who had returned to India and Bhutan for a retreat after five years of study at Oxford University and a new venture of teaching dharma to Westerners. Rinpoche's English would have been accented but comprehensible, and his curiosity about Christian monasticism was at its peak. Merton was visiting Asia to look for true spiritual masters about whom he had read for so many decades. He was later to admit to a special attraction to the spirituality of the Tibetans.

On Merton's first day in India, he and Rinpoche discovered each other over gin and tonics at the Central Hotel bar in Calcutta, talking about the contemplative life and its challenges in the twentieth century. It was the first of a number of conversations over the next couple of months in different parts of India. In his journals, Merton commented: "[T]he important thing is that we are people who have been waiting to meet for a long time. Chögyam Trungpa is a completely marvelous person. Young, natural, without front or artifice, deep, awake, wise. I am sure we will be seeing a lot more of each other" (AJ, 30). Rinpoche had a similar rapport with Merton. In the 1971 edition of his autobiography, he wrote: "Father Merton himself was an open, unguarded, and deep person. During these few days, we spent much time together and grew to like one another immensely. He proposed that we should collaborate on a book bringing together sacred writings of the Catholic and Vajra-yana Buddhist traditions."[1] In another reflection, Rinpoche commented, "Meeting Thomas Merton was wonderful; he was like a child, and at the same time, he was full of energy and life."[2] Still later, Rinpoche was to conclude: "I had the feeling that I was meeting an old friend, a genuine friend. . . . [Father Merton] was the first genuine person I met from the West."[3]

The conversations these two began that day were unusual in their intimacy, depth, and respect in a world where genuine inter-religious understanding was rare. They represented the opening and expanding of the boundaries of spirituality so that mutual inquiry and deep listening might engender a more universal and unbiased view, transforming both. Thirteen years later, in the 1980s, Chögyam Trungpa Rinpoche launched a series of seven landmark dialogue conferences at the fledgling university he had founded, Naropa Institute in Boulder, Colorado. From the beginning, Rinpoche dedicated these gatherings to "Father Merton" and said that he sought to cultivate the kind of conversations between genuine contemplatives that he had discovered with Merton.[4] Since that time, Naropa University has cherished dialogue as essential to its mission.

On the morning of his untimely death, in his talk on Marxism and monasticism delivered at the Benedictine conference in Bangkok, Merton spoke enthusiastically of Trungpa Rinpoche, referring to him as "a good friend of mine—a very interesting person indeed," and he expressed a desire to visit him later in Scotland (*AJ*, 337–38). Rinpoche was deeply saddened by Merton's premature death, feeling he had lost a heart friend, a genuine dialogue partner.

Because of his Trappist solitude, prior to his Asian journey Merton's dialogues were conducted almost entirely through correspondence. During his years in his hermitage at Gethsemani, Merton carried on vital conversations—most often by letter—with religious peers from many traditions. He had intimate exchanges with Zen exponent D. T. Suzuki, feminist theologian Rosemary Ruether, Vietnamese monk Thich Nhat Hanh, Rabbi Zalman Schachter, Sufi master Abdul Aziz, Taoist teacher John C. W.

Hu, and Hindu author Amiya Chakravarty. He yearned to travel
to actually meet contemplatives on their own soil, in their own
hermitages and temples, and to learn of their inner lives. When
his abbot finally granted permission for him to travel to Asia, he
confessed his joy "of being at last on my true way after years of
waiting and wondering and fooling around" (*AJ*, 4).

A few days after Merton's rendezvous with Chögyam Trungpa,
he joined the interreligious Spiritual Summit Conference to which
he had been invited, sponsored by the Temple of Understanding,
held at Birla Academy in South Calcutta. He had prepared remarks
in advance, reflecting the trajectory of his work and dialogues up
until 1968; these are published as "Monastic Experience and East-
West Dialogue" in appendix IV in *The Asian Journal*. Later, Merton
confessed that at the summit he "did not follow [his] prepared
text," and the paper was not actually delivered. But these prepared
remarks provide a window on the intention and experience of dialogue that he and Trungpa Rinpoche shared in Calcutta and later
in Delhi, and they provide a blueprint for a new kind of dialogue.
I have always appreciated this little essay as a set of guidelines for
the dialogue of practice, and imagine they reflect the conversations
in the Central Hotel bar.

First, Merton suggested that we enter dialogue as "pilgrims,"
not as research scholars or polemicists. When Merton went to
Asia, he was eager to encounter spiritual masters of Hinduism and
Buddhism in order to expand and deepen his own spirituality. He
was especially interested in learning meditation and contemplation
directly, mind to mind, from the adepts themselves.

In dialogue, we explore our inner depths while encountering
the religious other. Merton wished to "drink from ancient sources
of monastic vision and experience . . . to become a better and more
enlightened monk (qualitatively) myself" (*AJ*, 313). This journey
requires what Merton called "spiritual maturity," in which the pilgrim remains open and inquisitive even while deepening her roots

in the sources of her own tradition. An openness to "conversion" in dialogue does not necessarily mean forsaking our own spiritual heritage.

The journey of dialogue, however, is perilous, Merton teaches. He acknowledged that we cannot know the outcome of our pilgrimage, which often takes us beyond the limits of tradition. Dialogue requires "being wide open to life and to new experience because [we have] fully utilized [our] own tradition and gone beyond it" (*AJ*, 315). Pilgrimage works on a "postverbal" level, so that we can meet "beyond [our] own words and [our] own understanding in the silence of an ultimate experience which might conceivably not have occurred if [we] had not met and spoken" (*AJ*, 315). The primary focus is on the journey and the heart of spiritual vocation.

When considering the "contemplative life," Merton did not necessarily mean monasticism. By 1958, he had come to understand that living in the monastery was not contemplative for everyone. He also indicated in his correspondence with laypeople throughout the world that the contemplative life could be lived surrounded by the trappings of home, family, and livelihood. Merton redefined the contemplative life to mean "a certain distance or detachment from the 'ordinary' and 'secular' concerns of worldly life," which he defined as monastic solitude. He also wrote of "preoccupation with the radical inner depth" and "concern with inner transformation." This transformation entails the "eventual breakthrough and discovery of a transcendent dimension of life beyond that of the ordinary empirical self and of ethical and pious observance" (*AJ*, 309–10).

Merton adds the importance of community practice, for it is in community that we learn that the contemplative life can never be only for oneself or by oneself. Our communities teach us authenticity and where our blind spots are, and they train us in humility. They introduce us to daily practice beyond dogma and platitude. They also pull us out of our self-preoccupations and show us that our humanity and vocation require that we serve the world. Dialogue is another way that we move out into that larger world in service and humbleness. As contemplatives, we "seek to penetrate the ultimate ground of [our] beliefs by a transformation of the religious consciousness" (*AJ*, 311). The dialogue of practice requires openness to this ultimate ground in the life of our dialogue partner in order to test and stretch our own ultimate ground.

"Scrupulous respect" for genuine differences is a foundation of deep dialogue: "There are differences that are not debatable, and it is a useless, silly temptation to try to argue them out. Let them be left intact until a moment of greater understanding." In this encounter, however, we must overcome the temptation of falling into syncretism, dismissing or collapsing the integrity of the individual traditions themselves. There is much in our contemporary environment that would have dismayed Merton—"a mishmash of semireligious verbiage and pieties, a devotionalism that admits everything and therefore takes nothing with full seriousness." This highlights the importance for contemplative dialogue partners to be rooted in their own traditions, deeply practiced and trained. It is clear that he valued "authentic contact with the past of [our] own community," which I take to be classical contemplative training (*AJ*, 311, 316).

For me, Merton's inspiration, also shared by my Tibetan Buddhist teacher, has brought a new and refreshing dimension into my spiritual life based on the intersubjectivity of inquiry and dialogue. When encountering a religious or spiritual other, I have discovered that together we are able to surface unacknowledged parts of ourselves and listen to these voices. This journey requires tremendous openness that is the foundation of genuine dialogue. My friend and longtime dialogue partner, Brother Gregory Perron, O.S.B., who lives a life profoundly influenced by Merton, describes intrareligious dialogue as "listening dangerously" to the inner voices of our multiple religious identities, finding wisdom in each of them, and drawing sustenance for our human personhood that transcends any of them. This unfolding journey of discovery yields an inner depth that transforms an ordinary conversation into what Brother Gregory calls a "spiritual adventure."[5]

I have found that listening to these sometimes-disparate voices is only the beginning. We are challenged to suspend judgment and respect what we hear. While in dialogue with an evangelical, we can listen deeply to the evangelical voice inside ourselves, allow it to speak, respect its integrity, and suspend judgment—and something powerful happens. When encountering the moralist, we find to our surprise a moralist lives within us as well. When we truly listen to another, a resonance opens in our hearts, even if we have a conceptual reaction that closes doors between us; it is the human connection that speaks to us. If we are committed to suspending judgment, we find ourselves listening deeply. That listening leads us to hearing our own hearts as well, and we begin to recognize the orphaned identities we carry. When we can integrate all of these identities into our deepest knowing, our spiritual journeys blossom. The spiritual life has potential I never dreamed of!

When Thomas Merton and Chögyam Trungpa met in the Central Hotel bar in 1968, they could not have known the impact of their conversations on the generations to follow. While their plans to work together in the future were not to materialize, the inspiration of their exchange deeply influenced the young tulku who was to be pivotal in the generation of dharma in the West. The Buddhist-Christian dialogues Rinpoche launched at Naropa Institute in 1981 came uniquely from a visionary Buddhist contemplative rather than a Christian one. They enacted in a public but intimate setting conversations that previously had been private and informal. They revitalized the inner lives of the presenters and participants for years to come. And they embossed into the foundation of my little Buddhist university in Colorado the wider vision of religious pluralism, contemplative exchange, and the dialogue of practice.

9.
The Dazzling Light Within

Ilia Delio, O.S.F.

The monastic life is based on stability. The Rule of St. Benedict admonishes the monk not to leave the monastery, that is, not to wander from place to place but to remain in one's cell and meditate on God. So it was quite an unusual day in 1958 when Thomas Merton, a Trappist monk who achieved fame by his autobiography *The Seven Storey Mountain*, found himself standing at the intersection of a busy corner in downtown Louisville, Kentucky.

What was a Trappist monk doing in the midst of a busy city? He was on a simple errand; but, in a way that he himself could never fully explain, Merton was drawn into the heart of the world when, in the center of a shopping district, he realized that he and all the people around him were deeply united, a unity that he experienced as a strong bond of love: "I was suddenly overwhelmed with the realization that I loved all those people, that they were mine and I theirs, that we could not be alien to one another even

though we were total strangers" (*CGB*, 155). How did a man who
was removed from the world find himself deeply united to all people in the world? More so, why do we who are in the world find
ourselves separated from one another, as if we *do not* share the same
humanity? I think the key to Merton's cosmic sense of union lies in
his search for true identity and the source of his identity in God.

Often we think of ourselves as finished products, as if God
created us and then disappeared. The spiritual writer Beatrice
Bruteau realized how short-sighted this thinking can be. The "I" is
not a finished product, she wrote, something left over from God's
creative activity; rather, it is the very process of God's creative
action. Merton too had something of this idea when he said that
"the secret of my identity is hidden in the love and mercy of God"
(*NSC*, 35). To know this truth, Merton wrote, we are to "pray for
our own discovery."

Such advice seems counterproductive in an age of holistic
healing, depth psychology, and artificial intelligence. Yet Merton
understood that, despite our incredible advances in science and
technology, nothing can replace the power of prayer. Prayer is that
deep dialogue with God, a heart-to-heart encounter in which the
innermost center of our being continuously stretches toward that
which is not yet seen and longs for that which is not yet known.
Contrary to popular belief, prayer is not so much what we do but
what we become when we open up to God.

It was said of Francis of Assisi that he did not so much pray as
he himself became living prayer. In prayer, we are confronted by
our most fundamental meaning of existence, to radiate the presence of God. Most people do not see themselves as the dwelling
place of God, but this is precisely the profound dignity of the
human person. As Merton claimed, "God utters me like a word
containing a partial thought of Himself" (*NSC*, 37). Imagine if
we awoke every morning by saying, "I am God's thought today."
God's life and my life are intertwined, like a DNA double helix.

Prayer is coming to a deeper consciousness of our lives intertwined with God's life. For this reason, prayer is the path to our true self, wherein lies our happiness. The more we avoid prayer and finding our true self in God, the more we are imprisoned by an illusory self that is unfree: "This true inner self must be drawn up like a jewel from the bottom of the sea, rescued from confusion, from indistinction, from immersion in the common, the nondescript, the trivial, the sordid, the evanescent. We must be saved above all from that abyss of confusion and absurdity which is our own worldly self. The person must be rescued from the individual" (*NSC*, 38).

Merton's search for the true self in God contradicts our culture of self-making and constructed identities, especially the fluid construction of personal profiles on social media sites that can be changed with the touch of a button. In Merton's view, no technology can help us find the truth of our identity because the search for the true self is our ongoing relationship with God, and this relationship is an ever deepening of love. It is a type of self-discovery that cannot be found in books, self-help programs, or degree programs. The truth of our identity is found in detaching ourselves from ourselves in order to see all things in God.

Much of our culture today is geared toward creating the illusion of a false self, the self we think we need to be in order to be happy. Pursuing this false self is the greatest obstacle to our happiness because God knows nothing of this self. God did not create it—we did. In Merton's view, we need to unplug from everything that prevents relationship with God and turn our attention to sharing with God the work of *creating* the truth of our identity. This is our vocation, "not simply to *be*, but to work together with God in the creation of our own life" (*NSC*, 32). Every person has something vital to contribute to the world, something unique, flowing from the personal gift of one's life. Sometimes the gift is the gift of presence or laughter or sharing a story. It is not so much what we do that builds the world but how we love—and every person is gifted in love.

Merton thought that to live the truth of our own existence is to be a saint. A tree is holy, he wrote, simply by being a tree; flowers are saints gazing up into the face of God. We humans are no less called to be ourselves and in being ourselves to radiate the glory of God. However, very few people grasp the holiness of their lives. Rather, there is an implicit belief that God is watching from above and that we have to make our way to heaven to see God. Merton said, "we cannot go to heaven because we do not know where heaven is or what it is" (*NSC*, 39)—so God comes to us. God comes down from heaven and finds us, just as God sought Adam in the Garden of Eden (cf. Gn 3:9).

There is nothing we can do or say that can alienate God from our lives. We can disown God, but God cannot disown us because God cannot disown his own self (2 Tm 2:13). Merton described this inscrutable mystery when he said, "our discovery of God is, in a way, God's discovery of us." Our praying to God is God praying in us. Our lives and God's life are so intertwined that loving God is God loving God's own self in us! Prayer is waking up to this reality, coming to a new consciousness of God's indwelling presence. "We become contemplatives," Merton wrote, "when God discovers himself in us" (*NSC*, 39). So God does not desire that we become anything other than the truest self God has loved from all eternity. If we could discover this great mystery of God in us, we would be truly free, and out of this freedom we could build a new world of unity in love.

The search for true identity requires an honest self-love. Love of self is not selfishness but a humble recognition of our lives as true, good, and beautiful. Without real love of self, all other loves are distorted. Lack of self-knowledge, St. Bonaventure once wrote, makes for faulty knowledge in all other matters. Merton realized that so many people are weighed down by deep hurts, anger, resentment, lost loves, and broken relationships, desperately seeking to fill their lives with happiness and peace. As he himself was searching for truth and identity, he came to a deep insight—that each human person already has what they are looking for: the treasure is within. While our scientific age boasts of cloning and synthetic DNA, Merton said that there is a dazzling light at the heart of the human person that cannot be technologically manipulated because this light is the absolute brilliance of God:

> At the center of our being is a point of nothingness which is untouched by sin and by illusion, a point of pure truth, a point or spark which belongs entirely to God, which is never at our disposal, from which God disposes of our lives, which is inaccessible to the fantasies of our mind or the brutalities of our own will. This little point of nothingness and of absolute poverty is the pure glory of God in us. It is so to speak His name written in us, as our poverty, as our indigence, as our dependence, as our sonship. It is like a pure diamond, blazing with the invisible light of heaven. It is in everybody, and if we could see it we would see these billion points of light coming together in the face and blaze of a sun that would make all the darkness and cruelty of life vanish completely. (*CGB*, 156)

This dazzling light in the depth of the human person is the same dazzling light at the heart of our big bang universe, and if we could see this light, we would be at home with the stars, the galaxies, the planets, and all peoples. It seems so incredibly challenging—perhaps impossible—and yet, as Merton realized, it is so simple because this light is found in the stillness of solitude. As St. Augustine wrote centuries ago, "I was searching without but You were within." We are constantly looking outside ourselves for the dazzling light, but often we find darkness. For the light within us is invisible, like the breath of our lives. One could liken it to the story of the little fish in the sea who swam to its mother and said,

"Mommy, they were talking about this thing called 'water' today in school. We swam all around looking for it—from the bottom of the ocean to the place where the land meets the sea—but couldn't find it! Where is this thing called 'water?'"[1] Similarly, we can ask, where is this thing called "God"? Merton's answer is simple: God is not out there. We are already in God and God is in us. Yet we are constantly fishing for God—running from one event to another, one store to another, one person to another—and we cannot find what we are looking for.

Happiness, my mother once told me, is wanting what you already have. To make this discovery we need the quiet, inner space of solitude. Solitude is not being alone, but being alone with God. It is awakening to the inner dazzling light, realizing that, no matter what we do or where we are, we are not alone—God is with us, in us, loving us, freeing us, creating us, but will do nothing without our consent. When we begin to live in prayerful solitude, we begin to realize just how awesome is this God of love. We can find solitude in the midst of the forest or the midst of a mall. Merton was living in solitude when he experienced his oneness with all people on the corner of Fourth and Walnut Streets. Jesus lived from the solitude of oneness with God. "The Father and I are one," he said (Jn 10:30). Out of this deep oneness, the dazzling light of God shone through Jesus' life, and he experienced oneness with all people, whether Jew or Gentile, male or female, slave or free.

Physicist David Bohm once wrote, "as human beings and societies we seem separate but in our roots we are part of an indivisible whole and share in the same cosmic process."[2] Merton realized this wholeness on a street corner in downtown Louisville. We too are created to be part of a whole, the body of Christ, the body of all peoples, the body of the universe, of the stars and galaxies and all planetary life. The key to wholeness is in the truth of our identity, and this truth exists from all eternity in the love of God, a love that shines like an ever-burning flame within us. If we can find this love within and live from its radiance, we shall no longer be wandering in an alien world, for we shall know God heart-to-heart and see God face-to-face.

10.

False Self, True Self: Finding the Real Me

SUE MONK KIDD

I opened *New Seeds of Contemplation* for the first time during the winter of 1988 while visiting Thomas Merton's hermitage in the Kentucky woods about a mile from the Abbey of Gethsemani. I'd made several trips to the monastery, but this was my first to the small cinder-block house where Merton lived for the last few years of his life. I doubt there could be a more ideal location in which to read Merton's masterpiece on the contemplative life, but I'm pretty sure I could have read the book on a bench in a shopping mall and it would have affected me similarly—as an occasion of awe and awakening. As an event that changed me.

When I made my pilgrimage to the hermitage, I was thirty-nine years old, flailing about in a profusion of busyness, struggling to balance my roles as mother, wife, and writer and keep pace with what seemed like a preposterous assortment of demands. People were often surprised by my gravitation to monasteries. I joked to them that my maiden name was, after all, Monk, and they joked that I was just tired and wanted to go off somewhere and lie down.

My guide that day was a thin, amiable monk with horn-rimmed glasses. As we set off from the monastery through the empty trees, he inquired how I'd become interested in Merton.

"Reading *The Seven Storey Mountain*," I told him. When he smiled, I added, "That's practically a religious cliché, isn't it?"

I'd read the autobiographical account of Merton becoming a Trappist monk ten years earlier, at the age of twenty-nine. The book fairly stunned me. Having grown up in a Baptist family in a small town in the South, I'd had no religious orientation to the contemplative life, no idea about monasteries or what sort of infectious mystery might compel someone to actually go to one.

Merton himself wrote about literature that "initiates" the reader into "the ultimate cause of things," calling it "wisdom literature," and applying the term to the work of Faulkner, for one. It was easy for me to apply the term to *Seven Storey Mountain*. My experience of reading it initiated me into my first real awareness of the interior life, igniting an impulse toward being that I still felt a decade later.

I'd gone on to read other of Merton's books, mostly his published journals, but somehow, inexplicably, I hadn't yet read *New Seeds of Contemplation*, which was tucked in my purse, along with a small journal.

"So, for you, Merton was essentially a contemplative?" the monk said.

I nodded, startled slightly by the notion that Merton might be viewed as anything else. (Later I would wonder if that wasn't what my guide had in mind.) I'd understood Merton almost exclusively as a man drawn by prayer, solitude, and silence, the real essence of his life and work rooted in his pull toward being.

As I would discover, however, the light of Merton can be both wave and particle, one's vision of him highly influenced by one's own experience, need, and initiation. Merton was, in fact, multifaceted, complex, even self-contradictory, meaning he was able to hold within his extravagant personality a wide range of ambiguities, paradoxes, and selves. Out of the great fertility and imagination of his soul rose a contemplative, monk, hermit, writer, poet, artist, intellectual, cultural critic, dissident, peace activist, ecumenical seeker, lover of nature, and ordinary guy. A kind of Everysoul, he possessed an extraordinary ability to connect with deep, universal places inside of people. His life became a remarkably clear lens through which others glimpse their own self, especially the self their soul most demands. So, even before we reached the hermitage, it occurred to me I may have sculpted a personal image of Merton that had as much to do with my *own* longing to be, as it did with his.

The hermitage was enclosed by drifting floes of brown leaves, its cement-slab porch laden with firewood. I walked slowly through each room: a small kitchen; a bedroom with a quilt-draped bed pushed against the wall; a tiny room used for a chapel, its altar adorned with origami-shaped seed pods; and a living room with a fireplace, a shelf of books, a wooden rocker (was this where Jacques Maritain sat on his visit here?), walking sticks propped in a corner, and an oil lamp on a desk before the front window. It smelled heavily of woodsmoke.

With a stretch of time to myself, I settled at the desk and pulled *New Seeds of Contemplation* from my bag. In its pages I discovered Merton's powerful evocations on the true self.

"Our vocation is not simply to *be*, but to work together with God in the creation of our own life, our own identity, our own destiny . . . to work out our identity in God" (*NSC*, 32).

I've never attempted to describe the experience I had upon reading that passage. Even now, so many years later, I don't know what to say about it except that it caused something hidden at the core of me to flare up and become known. If my reading of *Seven*

Storey Mountain inducted me into the mysteries of the interior
life, waking an urge to be, *New Seeds of Contemplation* initiated
me into the secrets of my true identity and woke in me an urge
toward realness.

While seated at the desk, I copied a number of sentences from
the book into the journal, which I recently dug out of its long
obscurity in the back of a closet in order to read again. The lines
I chose to write down reveal my own subjective experience with
the book. They seem to me now like tiny panes through which I
can glimpse the intimate yearnings of an earlier self.

I copied this rather telling passage: "Every one of us is shadowed by an illusory person: a false self. . . . We are not very good
at recognizing illusions, least of all the ones we cherish about
ourselves" (*NSC*, 34).

And this one: "Contemplation is not and cannot be a function
of this external self. There is an irreducible opposition between the
deep transcendent self that awakens only in contemplation, and
the superficial, external self which we commonly identify with the
first person singular" (*NSC*, 7).

And this, which is written on a page by itself, surrounded by
astonished, blank space: "Our reality, our true self, is hidden in
what appears to us to be nothingness. . . . We can rise above this
unreality and recover our hidden identity" (*NSC*, 281).

"God himself . . . begins to live in me not only as my Creator,
but as my other and true self" (*NSC*, 41).

My last excerpt captured the polarity I felt inside: "We have
the choice of two identities: the external mask which seems to
be real . . . and the hidden, inner person who seems to us to be
nothing, but who can give himself eternally to the truth in whom
he subsists" (*NSC*, 295).

As I read, my understanding of Merton and the spiritual
life began to pivot. Who am I? Who is my real self? How shall
I become that self? The questions suddenly seemed to form the

nucleus of Merton, and somehow, the nucleus of me, too. The shift that occurred in me had to do with discovering an *intention* of contemplation previously unknown to me—the process of confronting the false self, the illusions and tenacity of the ego, and finding and surrendering to the true self. Merton poetically referred to it as a movement from opaqueness to transparency.

Again Merton's wisdom literature had taken me into the ultimate cause of things. The encounter has impacted my spirituality and my writing to this day.

Not long ago, as I retrieved the little journal containing the passages I'd inscribed, a photograph tumbled from inside the cover. It was a picture of me standing on the hermitage porch, burrowed in a white coat, looking something like a young novice. Gazing at it nearly twenty years later, I was struck by the realization that I'd read *New Seeds of Contemplation* several times since then, experiencing the book differently each time: as a classical theological work on the nature of contemplation, as a collection of personal meditations that tend the soul, and as a mystical vision of what Merton called the "cosmic dance." Yet I savor most that reading in 1988 when my first awareness of the true self appeared in the portal of a winter afternoon.

11.

Thomas Merton Is
a Dangerous Fellow

TIMOTHY MCCORMICK

I spent close to fifteen years actively avoiding Thomas Merton. The avoiding began in my early twenties when I started to take my faith seriously and then felt the call to full-time lay ministry. After college, I spent seven years as a college campus minister followed by eight years as a high school theology teacher, where I remain today. My interests early on were mainly in systematic theology and apologetics, with issues like spirituality, ecumenism, and interfaith dialogue taking a distant back seat. During that time, Merton's name was familiar to me, but back then the writers and commentators I was interested in reading were, on the whole, not all that complimentary toward him or his writings. (A quick online search even today shows the diversity of opinion about him.)

I remember doing Google searches on Merton at that time and finding something of a "two Mertons" theory being proposed. According to this view, the "first Merton" was the earlier of the two and was most often described as the "good" Merton, corresponding to the era of *The Seven Storey Mountain* and his early spiritual writings. He was the obedient monk who had an amazing conversion story and went on to write a number of solidly orthodox spiritual classics. However, this Merton did not last long—for there was also the "bad" or "misguided" Merton, who got swept up in the antiwar movement, social justice issues, and non-Christian religions during the 1960s up until his death. A number of commentators referred to these later writings of his as dangerous reading! I was even told by a person I did ministry with that if Merton hadn't died when he did, he would have probably ended up leaving the Church to become a Buddhist. Therefore the impression I got, which would stay with me for many years, was that Merton was dangerous or, at the very least, unsafe reading. For me, that was enough to avoid him completely.

My poorly informed view of this man changed a few years back when I finally decided to take a fresh look. To this day, I am not completely sure what motivated me. Perhaps it was a quote of Merton's being posted on social media that caught my attention, or it could have been seeing one of those classic photos of him either at prayer or staring reflectively into the camera. Maybe I was at a new stage of my own life, asking different questions and seeing the world a bit differently than before. Maybe I was ready to be a little dangerous. Or maybe it was simply the grace of God. All I knew was that I was open and hungry for something different. I wasn't being fed spiritually by what I had been reading at the time, or really for the years that preceded it. In fact, my prayer life had stopped growing.

Yet, even with this new openness, everything that I had been told previously made me wary at first. So I decided to proceed not by reading one of Merton's actual writings, but by ordering a short biography. Fortunately, there had been one published that same year that was just over one hundred pages in length. I figured that this would be perfect, since I could read the book in a couple of days, be confirmed in the suspicions I had harbored against him, and then move on to something else. Big mistake! First, it didn't take me a day or two to read the book, only a few hours. I devoured it, and all it did was make me hungry for more. Second, in reading about the life of Merton, I discovered a man of the twentieth century who spoke and wrote in my own language and not in translation, who was always striving for something and never felt settled. He was always curious. This appealed to me at that moment in my life. That is how *I* felt. Even with my graduate background in theology, I was still grappling with questions about God, suffering, and prayer. Most often, I would keep the questions to myself. The textbook answers I had been given were not satisfying anymore. It wasn't that I necessarily felt the answers given were wrong, but I didn't feel they made any practical difference to my actual lived experience I needed to, in a sense, experience the challenge of struggling with these issues, without there being any easy answers. As I read Merton, I found a man who didn't keep quiet about his questions and questing. Instead, he funneled his curiosity creatively into his many journals, articles, letters, and books.

Merton had struggles and setbacks—and I could relate to him. Yet even through his difficulties finding solitude, his tensions with his abbot, and his restlessness with the outside world, he remained joyful and full of humor. All of this endeared him to me. It was only slowly that I began to understand the story of this man, where he came from, and what he was searching for. After reading the biography, I immediately ordered *The Seven Storey Mountain*. As I soon discovered, this was only the beginning.

Soon after reading his autobiography and then *New Seeds of Contemplation*, I ordered *The Sign of Jonas*. I am convinced that if I hadn't come into contact with his journals, my relationship with Merton would have ended there and then. While I would

have certainly come to a greater appreciation of the man and lost
any fear I had of reading him, I would have likely just moved on
to something or someone else. The journals made the greatest
difference. The honesty he shares in them I found refreshing. He
was real. He made me laugh out loud at times. He made me stop,
midsentence, to consider what he had just written. Soon after
reading *The Sign of Jonas*, I purchased a pair of his journals that
were edited and released in the late 1990s. I found my enjoyment
in reading his journals ironic, since I had tried journaling myself on
a number of occasions without success. (I journal regularly now.)
Through the journals, I realized that there were not "two Mertons,"
but rather "many Mertons." His life was a constant pursuit of the
real, the true self, and that was something I was called to do as well.
His writings gave me permission to ask questions that I had once
considered settled. There was no need to be afraid of searching and
discovering where God was hidden in my life and in the lives of
others, particularly those who seemed so different from me. Topics
like nonviolence, the Desert Fathers, and Zen Buddhism, which
I would have shied away from only a few years ago, have helped
move me into being both more satisfied in my Catholicism, and
having a genuine openness to learn from the other.

Since finding Merton, I have begun a daily practice of contemplative prayer. It has transformed my relationship with God.
God seems much bigger and more loving than I could have ever
imagined. Growing up in a loving Catholic home and attending
CCD and high school religion classes, I was always taught that
"God loves you." To be honest, I usually didn't take that concept
all that seriously. It seemed nice, I guess, but it didn't impact me
in any significant way. With my reading of Merton, along with
getting a wonderful spiritual director, I am starting to understand
the transformational truth of that statement. Thomas Merton has
opened my heart to the reality of God's love in my life. Inspired
by this, I have encouraged my students to take time each day to

pray in silence. We have even practiced beginning each class day with two minutes of silence. Sometimes we are able to stretch it to five, with the majority of the class telling me that they look forward to this time. Imagine a classroom full of high school students spending two to five minutes, at the beginning of class, just sitting in silence, opening themselves to the voice of a loving God. Praise God!

Thank you, Thomas Merton. I am sorry I avoided you for so long. You are a dangerous fellow.

12.

Merton's Love
Affair with
the Unknown

Fr. John-Julian, O.J.N.

The clergy conference was, if I remember rightly, in 1962. Father Paul Wessinger, S.S.J.E., was the speaker, scheduled to present a review and commentary on a book that had recently been published: *New Seeds of Contemplation*, by Thomas Merton.

We Anglican/Episcopalian clergy had all generally heard something of this Trappist Merton—some had skimmed his autobiography, *The Seven Storey Mountain*—but few of us had given him much more than a quick look, and he was seldom taken very earnestly. What none of us had recognized or appreciated was that this was an obviously talented, literate twentieth-century monk propounding what had generally been unheard in the Church since the medieval translations of *The Cloud of Unknowing* and the

171

works of John of the Cross and Meister Eckhart. Here was a contemplative who was not willing to settle—as most of us had—for emotional satisfaction and intellectual contentment as the satisfactory fruits of prayer. Ours had been a faith that Merton himself once described as "the spurious 'faith' of everyday life, the human faith which is nothing but the passive acceptance of conventional opinion" (*NSC*, 12).

So, suddenly, in Merton we were confronted with a master who pressed us far beyond what we had always considered adequate—far beyond what we had even considered extreme—and even beyond what most of us could imagine as possible.

Father Paul began his talk by reading some of the first words in Merton's *New Seeds of Contemplation*: "[C]ontemplation . . . is a more profound depth of faith, a knowledge too deep to be grasped in images, in words, or even in clear concepts. . . . For in contemplation we know by 'unknowing.' Or, better, we know *beyond* all knowing" (*NSC*, 1–2). We were staggered by those words—some of us offended and critical, some simply uncomprehending, some confused, and some smitten by what we sensed intuitively was a truth that somehow—to use Merton's words—we had known forever without knowing it.

Merton wrote: "A soul is an immaterial thing. It is a principle of activity, it is an 'act,' a 'form,' an energizing principle, it is the life of the body, and it must also have a life of its own, but the life of the soul does not inhere in any physical material subject" (*SSM*, 109). This was a breakaway for most of us from engagement and involvement with physical things: a crucifix, a prayer desk, an icon, a rosary, even the words in scripture or a book of prayers.

Perhaps the hardest dimension of this contemplative "work" (as *The Cloud of Unknowing* named it) was the recognition that virtually every one of the comprehensions and interpretations of God's nature we had ever known was flawed and inadequate and that in the very hand of divine grace we would be driven far beyond ourselves, beyond the best that our world and our minds could offer, into the terra incognita that is the omnipresent, imperceptible panentheism in which we would discover that, as Merton says, "God is Being itself" (*SSM*, 189). In fact, God's own words to Moses are more deeply true than anything else we can even faintly imagine: "*Ehyeh Asher Ehyeh*"—"I am that I am." (My translation: "I am what IS.") To Moses, God self-defined as essence, rather than action—as "Being itself." And the spiritual implications of this one primal understanding are almost beyond comprehension: God can be "located" within all that has "being." Within anything that exists, there is God.

This shows the Incarnation in a much deeper light: it carries a clear, temporal implication of the underlying primal spiritual reality that God exists (and has always existed) within *all* humankind, indeed, within all creation—the Creator bonded with creation by sharing out the divine attribute of *being* itself with all that was made. Hence, there is no distance between humanity and God. There is no other place or other time where God dwells any more truly than in the here and now. A human seeking after God is like a fish seeking after the ocean, for since we are created emanations of God's own self—"images of God" (the Hebrew word can mean "shadows")—wherever we are, there is that shard that lies in us as created beings. Merton speaks of this dimension as "a vivid awareness of infinite Being at the roots of our own limited beings" so that "[w]e ourselves become [God's] echo and His answer" (*NSC*, 3).

The *Cloud of Unknowing* author spoke of the deep yearning and direction of the spirit for God as the only human act that can contribute to the grace-filled gift of a consciousness of divine union. It is not with the mind or the emotions that one can touch God, but with the will—a human "wanting mechanism"—bound to the intellect. As Merton put it, "Since God is a Spirit, and infinitely above all matter and all creation, the only complete union possible, between ourselves and Him, is in the order of intention, a union of wills and intellects in love, charity" (*SSM*, 407).

The important thing is that what is being called for in this reaching for God is not the imposition of some new spirituality, but the full manifestation of *what is already there* within our created nature. In this, Merton uses the metaphor of a crystal: "When a ray of light strikes a crystal, it gives a new quality to the crystal. And when God's infinitely disinterested love plays upon a human soul, the same kind of thing takes place. And that is the life called sanctifying grace. . . . [W]hen that light shines on [a soul], it becomes in a manner transformed into light and seems to lose its nature in the splendor of a higher nature" (*SSM*, 186).

As my own patroness, Dame Julian of Norwich (whom Merton called "the greatest English theologian"), put it, "The soul can do no more than seek, suffer, and trust."[1] And it is the *seeking* that is our primary responsibility—the willing, the wanting, the yearning, and the longing. It is this seeking, this intention, that ought to be the human's first priority—above all else.

But this quest for God is always qualified, because no ordinary human exercise or practice can bring one into clear awareness of God. "Unless [God] utters Himself in you, speaks His own name in the center of your soul, you will no more know Him than a stone knows the ground upon which it rests in its inertia. . . . We become contemplatives when God discovers Himself in us," writes Merton (*NSC*, 39). In contemplative prayer, it is God who is the actor, not us.

In fact, it is easy for us to overvalue ourselves in our spiritual exertions. Before we know it, "the clean peace of a will united to God becomes a complacency of a will that loves its own excellence" (*NSC*, 49). None of us can ever accurately appraise or evaluate our own spiritual growth—we can simply never know how good we are because serious spiritual development comes into consciousness only in the retrospective of many years, if ever. The very last person who is comfortably aware of her/his spiritual health or sanctity is the saint—who inevitably (and sincerely) denies all adulation from others.

And what may be the hardest aspect of the contemplative way is that on a practical level, it is a solitary way, because it lives so deeply within the soul that the experience can have no real meaning anywhere else. "For now, oh my God, it is to You alone that I can talk, because nobody else will understand" (*SSM*, 459). The life of a contemplative is by definition a secret life. Merton says plainly, "There can be no contemplation where there is no secret" (*NSC*, 83).

13.
Staunch Friendship for the Love of God

Rabbi David Zaslow

Rabbi Zalman Schachter-Shalomi (affectionately called Reb Zalman) was born in Poland in 1924. During World War II, he and his family were sent to a detention camp in Marseille before immigrating to the United States in 1941. He was ordained in the Chabad Lubavitch Hasidic community in Brooklyn. Reb Zalman was the founder of the Jewish Renewal movement, and by the end of his life he oversaw the ordination of more than two hundred rabbis, cantors, and rabbinic pastors. He died at the age of eighty-nine in 2014.

Rabbi Zalman Schachter-Shalomi's first letter to Thomas Merton in 1960 began with the salutation, "Dear Father Louis" (the name Merton was given as a priest). Merton's response, equally formal and tentative, began "Dear Rabbi Schachter." The next exchange of letters, a short time later, began "Dear Tom" and "Dear Zalman." Although the two had not met in person, it was clear they sensed an immediate spiritual familiarity, which would deepen over eight years as they shared their religious hopes, professional frustrations, and personal struggles. They became, as Reb Zalman described it, "staunch colleagues and friends."[1] By 1964, they expressed deep brotherly love for one another, their personal intimacy mirroring the love and intimacy they each shared with God.

Although the outward manifestations of their religious beliefs seemed far apart, these two were uniquely equipped as companions. From Christmas 1960 until Merton's untimely death in 1968, they journeyed light years across the divide between Catholicism and Judaism. Their friendship began before Vatican II, just fifteen years after the Holocaust, when both men were embedded in their respective orthodox and highly ordered religious worlds. At that time Reb Zalman was a rabbi in the Chabad Hasidic dynasty, ordained in 1947, and Father Louis had been ordained in the Trappist order in 1949.

In a letter dated February 15, 1962, Merton wrote to Zalman of his mystical understanding of the relationship between Christianity and Judaism. He wrote: "The suffering Servant is One: Christ, Israel. There is one wedding and one wedding feast, not two or five or six. There is one bride. There is one mystery, and the mystery of Israel and of the Church is ultimately to be revealed as One. As one great scandal maybe to a lot of people on both sides who have better things to do than come to the wedding" (*HGL*, 535). As a Christian theologian, Merton was one of a kind, bravely weaving an interfaith bridge into the emerging new paradigm.

The special light of Reb Zalman and Thomas Merton's bond emerged in the darkness of a world on the verge of nuclear war, in a nation enmeshed not only in a civil rights struggle but also in a growing involvement in Vietnam. While interfaith gatherings may be common today, in the early 1960s ecumenism was defined as Catholics dialoguing with Protestants—Jews and Buddhists were far from included. Merton and Zalman broke that mold as trailblazers in their respective faiths by studying and absorbing spiritual practices and wisdom from masters of Eastern religions, all the while dialoguing about how to reconcile a loving God with the suffering in the world

Both fans and critics might have called Merton a "Zen Catholic," since his spiritual explorations linked him to Buddhism, but he also explored Judaism, Taoism, Hinduism, Sufism, and beyond. But while Merton and Reb Zalman were certainly pioneers in interfaith dialogue, each was solidly rooted in his own traditional religious observances.

In his memoir, *My Life in Jewish Renewal,* Reb Zalman described it this way: "[T]he person who is at the growing edge of something—if he has a direct connection to the trunk of the tree—is safe. The trunk is mostly deadwood but it gives structure to the tree. The growing edge gives life to the tree, and the two of these must be together. I sense that Merton did not want to wreck that balance." Zalman finishes the chapter about his friendship with Merton by saying: "My friend Thomas Merton had large concerns. It is sad that he had to leave so early, because he was just getting into a stride where his ecumenism was so rich and so full."[2]

Although in the 1990s, a quarter century after Merton's death, Reb Zalman humorously introduced his students to the idea of being a "hyphenated Jew"—a so-called Jew-Bu, Hin-Jew, Sioux-Jew, or Sufi-Jew—neither he nor Merton was looking to merge their religion with other spiritual paths. They simply acknowledged the influence of other religions on their own faith, and boldly imported spiritual practices from other traditions, like meditation, into their Judaism and Catholicism. Merton, for instance, brought certain Zen practices into his Catholicism while Zalman imported aspects of the Sufi Zikr practice into Judaism.

Reb Zalman was known to say, "[T]he people I can talk to I can't pray with, and the people I can pray with I can't talk to." Although he could talk politics with people he worked with on civil rights, nuclear nonproliferation, and other political causes, they often lacked a devotional life or personal connection to God. On the other hand, his friends who were deeply religious, for whom prayer and devotion to God were central, were often people who did not share his political views. These were the ones he could pray with but could not talk to. When it came to Thomas Merton, though, Reb Zalman could both talk and pray with him, and they did—in letters, meetings, and in their exchange of favorite theological articles and books.

Their most intimate exchanges occurred during Zalman's extended visits to the Abbey of Gethsemani in Kentucky, where he took some of his own spiritual retreats. It was there that they—Zalman in his late thirties, Merton in his late forties—talked about God, prayed in English, Hebrew, and Latin, or just sat together in long periods of silence. Years later, Zalman told me he had received a letter in 1962 in which Merton said, "I have sat on the porch of the hermitage and sung chapters and chapters of the Prophets in Latin out over the valley, and it is a hair-raising experience is all I can say" (*HGL*, 535). This so inspired Zalman that on his next visit to the abbey, while sitting on the porch overlooking the Kentucky hills, he asked Merton to chant psalms in Latin while Zalman chanted them simultaneously in Hebrew. I imagine it must have been a doubly hair-raising experience.

By 1964, they were freely sharing the personal disappointments and frustrations that arose from their respective administrative duties, and the rigidity of some of the critics within their respective denominations. They both struggled to harmonize their spiritual calling as teachers within the limitations of the narrow thinking of some of their colleagues. In a fascinating exchange of letters starting February 6, 1964, Reb Zalman confided to Merton: "I can't describe to you the kind of rush I'm constantly under. . . . It is so difficult to think about G-d, always being his errand boy, then I say to myself: 'I didn't ask for the errand. It was sent to me.

Maybe he wants my errands more than my meditations.' So I will pray for you and please pray for me, and we will keep in mind . . . that whatever curve we get pitched will try to back. And after all, what is that business of the cross all about if not that?"[3] Merton responded on April 7 with a list of his own frustrations: "The usual weights and pressures, work . . . avalanche of meaningless yet necessary duties, and on top of that one of the brethren with misguided zeal denouncing me in a visitation, etc. Just the ordinary run of life, and I know you have much more of it than I have. . . . Let's keep one another in our prayers and may the Lord watch over us" (*HGL*, 539).

Another letter, dated February 13, 1964, has Zalman describing his relationship to Merton as like that of a lover, offering a mystical description of the kind of love they shared (some might call it agape love). He wrote, "[T]here may be something that is happening between you and me, right now, or that is happening between countless lovers, lovers may cling to each other in the fall in order to have at least one coordinate of warmth and assurances as it is in the tumble of love." In another letter dated December 1, 1966, Zalman finished with these words: "For the time being I have nothing more to say, I'm sending you only this one thought— Just, I love you!"[4] This kind of language is more common now between two men, but in the mid-1960s that sort of passionate exchange between a rabbi and a priest was unique.

Reb Zalman recounts how in the 1950s, before he met Merton, he imagined his relationship to Catholics would be with Jesuits, because their theological approach to devotion was similar to his. Zalman told the story of a conservative new pope being elected during the time of Ignatius of Loyola, the founder of the Jesuit order and innovator of a new method of meditation. With the new pope, Ignatius's disciples were concerned that the Jesuits might not survive. A disciple asked Ignatius what they would do if their order was disbanded. Ignatius responded, "Fifteen minutes in the oratory, the place of prayer, and it's all the same to me."[5]

Then Reb Zalman put the story in a Jewish context. He explained that when a person chants Psalm 16:8, "sh'viti Hashem l'negdi tamid" (I keep the Lord always before me), it is like entering into a spiritual oratory, and it brings the individual back into balance. He likened this chant to a "reset button" for the soul, especially in difficult circumstances, for when we realize that God is always present, there is nothing to fear. Rather than a sublimation or denial of grief, fear, or disappointment, this simply brings us back to a direct experience of the divine. This is not only what Ignatius meant by the "fifteen minutes of prayer, and it's all the same," but perhaps also what Zalman and Merton reminded each other of, simply by their presence in each other's life. As they recognized the image of God, manifest as the Beloved, in each other, it became sweet medicine, or a reset, for them in the context of their generation and their very different religions. In the midst of their uniquely deep, passionate work in the world, they lovingly called each other back to a universal center.

Notes

1. Becoming Who We Are, by James Martin, S.J.

1. Karl Rahner, *Karl Rahner: Spiritual Writings*, ed. Philip Endean (Maryknoll, NY: Orbis Books, 2004), 177.

2. Meeting Thomas Merton for the First Time, by Mary Neill, O.P.

1. Monica Furlong, *Merton: A Biography* (New York: Harper & Row, 1980), xviii.

2. From the essay "White Pebble," in *Thomas Merton: Selected Essays*, ed. Patrick F. O'Connell (Maryknoll, NY: Orbis Books, 2014), 3–4.

3. Thomas Merton, *My Argument with the Gestapo* (New York: New Directions, 1975), 160–61.

3. On Spiritual Exploration, by Robert Ellsberg

1. Patrick Hart and Jonathan Montaldo, eds., *The Intimate Merton: His Life from His Journals* (New York: HarperOne, 1999), 58–59.

2. Ibid., 127.

3. "The Root of War Is Fear," in Thomas Merton, *Passion for Peace: Reflections on War and Nonviolence* (New York: Crossroad, 2006), 26.

4. "A Devout Meditation in Memory of Adolf Eichmann," in Merton, *Passion for Peace*, 67–71.

5. Robert Daggy, ed., *Introductions East and West: The Foreign Prefaces of Thomas Merton* (Greensboro, NC: Unicorn Press, 1981), 45, 46.

6. Thomas Merton, *Life and Holiness* (New York: Herder and Herder, 1963), 21.

7. Pope Francis, Address to Joint Session of Congress, Washington, DC, September 24, 2015.

4. How to Be a Friend, by Gregory K. Hillis

1. Jim Forest, *The Root of War Is Fear: Thomas Merton's Advice to Peacemakers* (Maryknoll, NY: Orbis Books, 2016), 43.

2. In recent years, correspondence with James Laughlin, Czeslaw Milosz, Victor and Carolyn Hammer, Jean Leclercq, and Catherine De Hueck Doherty have also been published.

3. Naomi Burton Stone's unpublished letter from May 12, 1956, is in the archives of the Thomas Merton Center at Bellarmine University.

4. Forest, *The Root of War Is Fear*, 190, 191.

5. Ibid., 192, 196.

6. Personal communication with Jim Forest, March 9, 2017.

6. What It Means to Be a Person of Dialogue, by Daniel P. Horan, O.F.M.

1. Pope Francis, Address to Joint Session of Congress, Washington, DC, September 24, 2015.

2. Augustine, *Confessions*, trans. Henry Chadwick (New York: Oxford University Press, 1998), III.6.11.

3. Quoted in *Thomas Merton: Essential Writings*, ed. Christine M. Bochen (Maryknoll, NY: Orbis Books, 2000), 82.

4. Orlando O. Espín, "Grace and Humanness: A Hispanic Perspective," in *We Are a People! Initiatives in Hispanic American Theology*, ed. Roberto S. Goizueta (Minneapolis: Fortress Press, 1992), 143.

5. See Kathryn Tanner, *Theories of Culture: A New Agenda for Theology* (Minneapolis: Fortress Press, 1997), 25–27.

6. Patrick O'Connell, "Culture," in *The Thomas Merton Encyclopedia*, ed. William H. Shannon, Christine M. Bochen, and Patrick F. O'Connell (Maryknoll, NY: Orbis Books, 2002), 95. The next four quotes, also from O'Connell, are taken from this article at this page number.

7. See Vatican II documents *Nostra Aetate* ("Declaration on the Relations of the Church to Non-Christian Religions"), *Gaudium et Spes* ("Pastoral Constitution on the Church in the Modern World"), and *Unitatis Redintegratio* ("Decree on Ecumenism"), among others.

8. Pope Francis, Address to Joint Session of Congress.

9. I generally agree with David Givey, who writes, "The two social issues that Thomas Merton considered most urgent to Americans during the 1960s were war and racism." Givey, *The Social Thought of Thomas Merton: The Way of Nonviolence and Peace for the Future* (Winona, MN: Saint Mary's Press, 2009), 89.

10. James T. Baker, *Thomas Merton: Social Critic* (Lexington: University Press of Kentucky, 1971), 98.

11. See, for example, Thomas Merton, *The Nonviolent Alternative*, ed. Gordon Zahn (New York: Farrar, Straus & Giroux, 1971); Gordon Zahn, "Thomas Merton: Reluctant Pacifist," in *Thomas Merton: Prophet in the Belly of a Paradox*, ed. Gerald Twomey (New York: Paulist Press, 1978), 55–79; and Daniel P. Horan, "Becoming Instruments of Peace: How Francis and Merton Challenge Us to Live Today," in *The Franciscan Heart of Thomas Merton* (Notre Dame, IN: Ave Maria Press, 2014), 199–218.

12. See William Oliver Paulsell, ed., *Merton and the Protestant Tradition* (Louisville, KY: Fons Vitae, 2017).

13. See Gray Henry and Jonathan Montaldo, eds., *Merton and Hesychasm: The Prayer of the Heart and the Eastern Church* (Louisville, KY: Fons Vitae, 2003).

14. John Wu, letter to Merton, November 28, 1961 (Thomas Merton Center, Bellarmine University), as cited in William Apel, *Signs of Peace: The Interfaith Letters of Thomas Merton* (Maryknoll, NY: Orbis Books, 2006), xv; see also 47–63.

7. How We Understand Our Sexual Lives, by Kaya Oakes

1. Augustine, *Confessions*, trans. E. B. Pusey. Project Gutenberg digital edition.

2. Dorothy Day, *The Long Loneliness* (New York: HarperOne, 2009).

3. Dorothy Day, *All the Way to Heaven: The Selected Letters of Dorothy Day*, ed. Robert Ellsberg (New York: Image, 2012).

4. Michael Mott, *The Seven Mountains of Thomas Merton* (Boston: Houghton Mifflin, 1984), 80.

PART II: LIFE LESSONS IN THE LIGHT OF MERTON

2. How Thomas Merton and the Music of Keith Jarrett Changed My Life, by Kevin Burns

1. Furlong, *Merton: A Biography*, xix.
2. Mott, *The Seven Mountains of Thomas Merton*, 439.

8. Merton on the Spiritual Promise of Interreligious Dialogue, by Acharya Judith Simmer-Brown

1. Chögyam Trungpa, *The Collected Works of Chögyam Trungpa, Volume 1*, ed. Carolyn Gimian (Boston: Shambhala, 2004), 263.

2. Chögyam Trungpa, *Hinayana-Mahayana Seminary Transcripts, 1980* (Boulder: Vajradhatu Publications, 1981), 33.

3. Chögyam Trungpa, *The Collected Works of Chögyam Trungpa, Volume 3*, ed. Carolyn Gimian (Boston: Shambhala, 2004), 477.

4. The dialogues in these Naropa conferences were published in Susan Szpakowski, ed., *Speaking of Silence: Christians and Buddhists in Dialogue* (Halifax, NS: Vajradhatu Publications, 2005).

5. Br. Gregory Perron, O.S.B., "Listening to the Lion's Roar: Notes on an Interreligious Dialogue," *Monastic Interreligious Dialogue Journal* 74 (April 2005): 2.

9. The Dazzling Light Within, by Ilia Delio, O.S.F.

1. Albert Haase, O.F.M., *Swimming in the Sun: Discovering the Lord's Prayer with Francis of Assisi and Thomas Merton* (Cincinnati: St. Anthony Messenger Press, 1993), 16.

2. David Bohm, *Wholeness and the Implicate Order* (New York: Routledge and Kegan Paul, 1980), 5.

12. Merton's Love Affair with the Unknown, by Fr. John-Julian, O.J.N.

1. Thomas Merton, *Witness to Freedom: Letters of Thomas Merton in Times of Crisis*, ed. William Shannon (New York: Harcourt Brace, 1964), 43–44; Julian of Norwich, *Revelations*, 12, my translation.

13. Staunch Friendship for the Love of God, by Rabbi David Zaslow

1. Rabbi Zalman M. Schachter-Shalomi with Edward Hoffman, *My Life in Jewish Renewal: A Memoir* (Lanham, MD: Rowman & Littlefield, 2012), 155.

2. Ibid., 160, 163.

3. Unpublished letters from Zalman Schachter to Thomas Merton, Thomas Merton Center at Bellarmine University, Louisville, KY. Used with permission.

4. Ibid.

5. This is a version of what Reb Zalman said in an interview transcribed in *Merton and Judaism: Holiness in Words; Recognition, Repentance, and Renewal*, ed. Beatrice Bruteau (Louisville, KY: Fons Vitae, 2003), 301.

Selected Works of Thomas Merton Published since 1944

Each category is organized chronologically by publication date. The year listed is the first publication date of each work.

AUTOBIOGRAPHY, MEMOIR, JOURNALS, LETTERS

The Seven Storey Mountain. New York: Harcourt Brace, 1948.

The Sign of Jonas. New York: Harcourt Brace, 1953.

The Secular Journal of Thomas Merton. New York: Farrar, Straus & Cudahy, 1959.

Woods, Shore, and Desert: A Notebook. Santa Fe: Museum of New Mexico Press, 1982.

The Hidden Ground of Love: The Letters of Thomas Merton on Religious Experience and Social Concerns. Edited by William H. Shannon. New York: Farrar, Straus & Giroux, 1985.

A Vow of Conversation: Journals, 1964–1965. Edited by Naomi Burton Stone. New York: Farrar, Straus & Giroux, 1988.

The Road to Joy: The Letters of Thomas Merton to New and Old Friends. Edited by Robert E. Daggy. New York: Farrar, Straus & Giroux, 1989.

Thomas Merton in Alaska: The Alaskan Conferences, Journals, and Letters. New York: New Directions, 1989.

The School of Charity: The Letters of Thomas Merton on Religious Renewal and Spiritual Direction. Edited by Patrick Hart, O.C.S.O. New York: Farrar, Straus & Giroux, 1990.

The Courage for Truth: The Letters of Thomas Merton to Writers. Edited by Christine M. Bochen. New York: Farrar, Straus & Giroux, 1993.

Witness to Freedom: The Letters of Thomas Merton in Times of Crisis. Edited by William H. Shannon. New York: Farrar, Straus & Giroux, 1994.

Run to the Mountain: The Story of a Vocation (The Journals of Thomas Merton, Volume 1: 1939–1941). Edited by Patrick Hart, O.C.S.O. San Francisco: HarperSanFrancisco, 1995.

Entering the Silence: Becoming a Monk and Writer (The Journals of Thomas Merton, Volume 2: 1941–1952). Edited by Jonathan Montaldo. San Francisco: HarperSanFrancisco, 1996.

A Search for Solitude: Pursuing the Monk's True Life (The Journals of Thomas Merton, Volume 3: 1952–1960). Edited by Lawrence S. Cunningham. San Francisco: HarperSanFrancisco, 1996.

Turning toward the World: The Pivotal Years (The Journals of Thomas Merton, Volume 4: 1960–1963). Edited by Victor A. Kramer. San Francisco: HarperSanFrancisco, 1996.

Dancing in the Water of Life: Seeking Peace in the Hermitage (The Journals of Thomas Merton, Volume 5: 1963–1965). Edited by Robert E. Daggy. San Francisco: HarperSanFrancisco, 1997.

Learning to Love: Exploring Solitude and Freedom (*The Journals of Thomas Merton, Volume 6: 1966–1967*). Edited by Christine M. Bochen. San Francisco: HarperSanFrancisco, 1997.

The Other Side of the Mountain: The End of the Journey (*The Journals of Thomas Merton, Volume 7: 1967–1968*). Edited by Patrick Hart, O.C.S.O. San Francisco: HarperSanFrancisco, 1998.

SPIRITUALITY, CONTEMPLATION, MYSTICISM

Seeds of Contemplation. Norfolk, CT: New Directions, 1949.

The Ascent to Truth. New York: Harcourt Brace, 1951.

No Man Is an Island. New York: Harcourt Brace, 1955.

The Silent Life. New York: Farrar, Straus & Cudahy, 1957.

Thoughts in Solitude. New York: Farrar, Straus & Cudahy, 1958.

Disputed Questions. New York: Farrar, Straus & Cudahy, 1960.

The Wisdom of the Desert: Sayings from the Desert Fathers of the Fourth Century. New York: New Directions, 1960.

The New Man. New York: Farrar, Straus & Cudahy, 1961.

New Seeds of Contemplation. Norfolk, CT: New Directions, 1961.

Life and Holiness. New York: Herder and Herder, 1963.

Contemplation in a World of Action. New York: Doubleday, 1971.

Love and Living. Edited by Naomi Burton Stone and Patrick Hart, O.C.S.O. New York: Farrar, Straus & Giroux, 1979.

Dialogues with Silence: Prayers and Drawings. Edited by Jonathan Montaldo. New York: HarperCollins, 2001.

The Inner Experience: Notes on Contemplation. Edited by William H. Shannon. New York: HarperCollins, 2003.

A Course in Christian Mysticism. Edited by Jon M. Sweeney. Collegeville, MN: Liturgical Press, 2017.

EASTERN THOUGHT

The Way of Chuang Tzu. New York: New Directions, 1965.

Mystics and Zen Masters. New York: Farrar, Straus & Giroux, 1967.

Zen and the Birds of Appetite. New York: New Directions, 1968.

The Asian Journal of Thomas Merton. Edited by Naomi Stone, Patrick Hart, O.C.S.O., and James Laughlin. New York: New Directions, 1973.

Merton & Sufism: A Complete Compendium. Edited by Rob Baker and Gray Henry. Louisville, KY: Fons Vitae, 1999.

Merton & the Tao: Dialogues with John Wu and the Ancient Sages. Edited by Cristóbal Serrán-Pagán y Fuentes. Louisville, KY: Fons Vitae, 2013.

WRITINGS ON WAR, PEACE, AND JUSTICE IN THE 1960S

The Behavior of Titans. New York: New Directions, 1961.

Seeds of Destruction. New York: Farrar, Straus & Giroux, 1964.

Gandhi on Non-Violence. New York: New Directions, 1965.

Conjectures of a Guilty Bystander. New York: Doubleday, 1966.

Raids on the Unspeakable. New York: New Directions, 1966.

Faith and Violence. Notre Dame, IN: University of Notre Dame Press, 1968.

The Nonviolent Alternative. Edited by Gordon C. Zahn. New York: Farrar, Straus & Giroux, 1980.

BIOGRAPHIES OF SAINTS AND CISTERCIAN HISTORY AND SPIRITUALITY

Exile Ends in Glory: The Life of a Trappistine, Mother M. Berchmans, O.C.S.O. Milwaukee: Bruce Publishing, 1948.

The Waters of Siloe. New York: Harcourt Brace, 1949.

What Are These Wounds? The Life of a Cistercian Mystic, Saint Lutgarde of Aywières. Milwaukee: Bruce Publishing, 1950.

The Last of the Fathers: Saint Bernard of Clairvaux and the Encyclical Letter, Doctor Mellifluus. New York: Harcourt Brace, 1954.

The Spirit of Simplicity, with Jean-Baptiste Chautard, O.C.S.O. Notre Dame, IN: Ave Maria Press, 2017.

LITERARY CRITICISM

The Literary Essays of Thomas Merton. Edited by Patrick Hart, O.C.S.O. New York: New Directions, 1981.

FICTION

My Argument with the Gestapo: A Macaronic Journal. New York: Doubleday, 1969.

POETRY

Thirty Poems. Norfolk, CT: New Directions, 1944.

A Man in the Divided Sea. Norfolk, CT: New Directions, 1946.

The Tears of the Blind Lions. Norfolk, CT: New Directions, 1949.

The Strange Islands: Poems. Norfolk, CT: New Directions, 1956.

Selected Poems. Norfolk, CT: New Directions, 1959.

Emblems of a Season of Fury. New York: New Directions, 1963.

Cables to the Ace. New York: New Directions, 1968.

The Geography of Lograire. New York: New Directions, 1969.

The Collected Poems of Thomas Merton. New York: New Directions, 1977.

Monk's Pond: Thomas Merton's Little Magazine, introduction by Robert E. Daggy. Lexington, KY: University Press of Kentucky, 1989.

The Contributors

Robert Barron is founder of Word on Fire Catholic Ministries and host of *Catholicism*, a groundbreaking, award-winning documentary about the Catholic faith. He is auxiliary bishop of the Archdiocese of Los Angeles.

Sylvia Boorstein, PhD, is author of *That's Funny You Don't Look Buddhist, Happiness Is an Inside Job*, and many other books.

Kevin Burns is coauthor, with Michael W. Higgins, of *Genius Born of Anguish: The Life and Legacy of Henri Nouwen*, and author of *Henri Nouwen: His Life and Spirit*.

Ilia Delio, O.S.F., holds the Josephine C. Connelly Endowed Chair in Theology at Villanova University. She is author of *The Unbearable Wholeness of Being, Making All Things New*, and many other books.

Robert Ellsberg is editor-in-chief of Orbis Books and editor of *All the Way to Heaven: The Selected Letters of Dorothy Day*.

Gregory K. Hillis, PhD, is associate professor of theology at Bellarmine University in Louisville, Kentucky. He regularly writes on theology and spirituality on his blog, myunquietheart.blogspot.com.

Daniel P. Horan, O.F.M., is a Franciscan priest and scholar who teaches at Catholic Theological Union in Chicago and author of *The Franciscan Heart of Thomas Merton, God Is Not Fair and Other Reasons for Gratitude*, and other books.

Kevin Hunt, O.C.S.O. Sensei, has been a monk of St. Joseph's Abbey in Spencer, Massachusetts, for more than fifty years. He was certified as a teacher of Zen in 2005 by Roshi Robert Jinsen Kennedy.

Paula Huston, a National Endowment for the Arts fellow, wrote literary fiction for more than twenty years before shifting her focus to spirituality. She's the award-winning author of several nonfiction books, including *Simplifying the Soul* and *One Ordinary Sunday*.

Pico Iyer is the author of many books about crossing cultures, including *Video Night in Kathmandu*. He publishes regularly in *Harper's*, the *New York Review of Books*, and the *New York Times*. His most recent book is *The Art of Stillness*.

Fr. John-Julian, O.J.N., served parishes in three states and was the founding dean of the Seminary of the Streets in New York before founding the Order of Julian in Wisconsin. He is author and translator of *The Complete Julian of Norwich* and other books.

Sue Monk Kidd's novel *The Secret Life of Bees* spent more than one hundred weeks on the *New York Times* Best Seller list, and has sold nearly six million copies.

James Martin, S.J., is editor-at-large of *America* magazine and the *New York Times* Best-Selling author of several books, including *The Jesuit Guide to (Almost) Everything* and *Jesus: A Pilgrimage*.

Timothy McCormick lives in suburban Detroit, where he works as a theology teacher at Bishop Foley Catholic High School. He holds an AS in Religious Education from St. Francis University and the STB from Sacred Heart Major Seminary.

Rabbi Phil Miller is retired vice president of the Jewish Community Center of Greater Baltimore. He is a graduate of Yeshiva University in New York City.

Mary Neill, O.P., is professor emerita and winner of the Distinguished Teaching Award at the University of San Francisco. She has coauthored four books on spirituality and frequently offers workshops and retreats in the Bay Area.

Kaya Oakes teaches creative nonfiction, literary journalism, research, and expository writing at the University of California, Berkeley, and is author of *The Nones Are Alright: A New Generation of Believers, Seekers, and Those in Between.*

Br. Paul Quenon, O.C.S.O., has been a monk at the Abbey of Our Lady of Gethsemani in Kentucky since Thomas Merton was novice master. He is a poet and photographer, and author of *Unquiet Vigil: New and Selected Poems.*

Acharya Judith Simmer-Brown, PhD, is Distinguished Professor of Contemplative and Religious Studies at Naropa University in Boulder, Colorado. She is an acharya (senior dharma teacher) of the Shambhala Buddhist lineage of Sakyong Mipham Rinpoche and Chögyam Trungpa Rinpoche, and has been active in Buddhist-Christian dialogue for decades.

Rabbi David Zaslow has been the spiritual leader of Havurah Shir Hadash synagogue in Ashland, Oregon, since 1996. His book *Jesus: First-Century Rabbi* won the Church & Synagogue Library Association's Book of the Year award.

Jon M. Sweeney is an independent scholar and one of religion's most respected writers. His work has been hailed by everyone from PBS and James Martin, S.J., to Fox News and Dan Savage. He's been interviewed on CBS *Saturday Morning*, Fox News, CBS-TV Chicago, *Religion and Ethics Newsweekly*, and on the popular program *Chicago Tonight*. Several of his books have become Book-of-the-Month Club and Quality Paperback Book Club selections. His popular medieval history, *The Pope Who Quit*, was published by Image/Random House and optioned by HBO. It was a selection of the History Book Club and received a starred review in *Booklist*. His book, *When Saint Francis Saved the Church*, received a 2015 award for excellence in history from the Catholic Press Association. His other works include *The Enthusiast*, *The Complete Francis of Assisi*, and *The St. Francis Prayer Book*. He was the editor of *A Course in Christian Mysticism* by Thomas Merton. Sweeney writes regularly for *America* and *The Tablet*, and is the publisher and editor-in-chief at Paraclete Press. He lives with his wife and two daughters in Milwaukee, Wisconsin.

AVE MARIA PRESS

Founded in 1865, Ave Maria Press,
a ministry of the Congregation of
Holy Cross, is a Catholic publishing
company that serves the spiritual and
formative needs of the Church and its
schools, institutions, and ministers;
Christian individuals and families; and
others seeking spiritual nourishment.

———————

For a complete listing of titles from

Ave Maria Press

Sorin Books

Forest of Peace

Christian Classics

visit avemariapress.com